THE CLASSICS OF WESTERN SPIRITUALITY
A Library of the Great Spiritual Masters

ATHANASIUS

THE LIFE OF ANTONY
AND
THE LETTER TO MARCELLINUS

TRANSLATION AND INTRODUCTION
BY
ROBERT C. GREGG

PREFACE
BY
WILLIAM A. CLEBSCH

PAULIST PRESS
NEW YORK • RAMSEY • TORONTO

Cover Art
A graduate of The Pennsylvania Academy of the Fine Arts in Philadelphia, cover artist
ANDRIJ MADAY has won numerous awards for his graphic designs and prints. He has
exhibited his paintings and woodcuts in approximately eighty shows in the United
States and has permanent collections at universities in Italy, Canada, and the United
States. Mr. Maday's art, based on simple rectangular and circular designs, is inspired by
ancient Ukranian icons and conveys Mr. Maday's own deep mystical experience and rich
Ukranian Eastern Orthodox heritage.

Design: Barbini, Pesce & Noble, Inc.

Library of Congress
Catalog Card Number: 79-56622

ISBN: 0-8091-2295-2 (paper)
       0-8091-0309-5 (cloth)

Published by Paulist Press
Editorial Office: 1865 Broadway, New York, N.Y. 10023
Business Office: 545 Island Road, Ramsey, N.J. 07446

Printed and bound in the United States of America

Contents

Author of the Preface

WILLIAM A. CLEBSCH, born in Clarksville, Tennessee, in 1923, studied at the University of Tennessee, Virginia Theological Seminary, Michigan State University, Union Theological Seminary, and Cambridge University. At Stanford University since 1964, he has held teaching and administrative responsibilities in Religious Studies, Humanities, and American Studies, becoming in 1979 the George Edwin Burnell Professor of Religious Studies and Professor of Humanities. He has written widely on topics in European and American religious history; recent books are *American Religious Thought, a History* (University of Chicago Press, 1973) and *Christianity in European History* (Oxford University Press, 1979). Both these books were written on senior fellowships from the National Endowment for the Humanities, respectively at Yale University and the University of North Carolina in Chapel Hill. He was named for 1980-81 a Fellow in Residence of the Center for Advanced Study in the Behavioral Sciences.

His earlier books include *England's Earliest Protestants, 1520-1535* (Yale University Press, 1964), *Pastoral Care in Historical Perspective* (with Charles R. Jaekle; editions in 1964, 1967, 1975), and *From Sacred to Profane America: The Role of Religion in American History* (Harper & Row, 1968).

In 1973 he was President of the American Society of Church History, and in 1979 chaired the jury for that society's first Philip Schaff Prize for the outstanding contribution to the history of Christianity from the North American scholarly community during 1977-78. He was elected in 1977 Vice-President, in 1978 President-elect, and in 1979 President of the American Academy of Religion.

At Stanford he has taken an active role in University governance, serving for many years on the Faculty Senate, including a year as its second chairman, and on the University Advisory Board. In 1979 he joined the Board of Visitors of Tulane University.

The Editor of this Volume

Born in February, 1938 in Kansas City, Missouri, ROBERT CLARK GREGG holds a B.A. from the University of the South, an S.T.B. from Episcopal Divinity School in Cambridge, Massachusetts, and a Ph.D. from the University of Pennsylvania.

From 1971 to 1974 Dr. Gregg was Assistant Professor of New Testament and Patristic Studies at Seabury Western Theological Seminary in Evanston, Illinois. Currently he is Associate Professor of Patristics and Medieval Church History in The Divinity School, Duke University.

Dr. Gregg's publications include *Consolation Philosophy: Greek and Christian Paideia in Basil and the Two Gregories* (No. 3 in the Patristic Monograph Series) and several articles written for scholarly journals. In collaboration with Dr. Dennis Groh, Dr. Gregg is currently writing a book on the religion and politics of the Arian controversy of the fourth century. He has also presented papers at the American Academy of Religion (1977), the North American Patristics Society (1974), the Oxford Patristics Conference (1975) and the American Society of Church History (1976). A member of the American Society of Church History and the North American Patristics Society, Professor Gregg is Executive Editor of the Philadelphia Patristics Foundation.

Dr. Gregg lives in Chapel Hill, North Carolina with his wife, Mary, and their four children, Clark, Andrew, Courtney, and Amy.

Acknowledgments

For their assistance in the preparation of this volume I wish to express my gratitude to five persons. James R. Mueller, while fully occupied by his studies at Duke, joined me in my labor over the Greek text, particularly the *Letter to Marcellinus.* Franklin Young was, as always, generous with his help in unlocking problematic passages, and in making me alert to nuances in the prose of Athanasius. Roland Murphy aided in the assessment of several theses advanced by Athanasius about the distinctiveness of the Psalter. Once again, Jacquelyn Norris transformed my hand-written manuscript into something intelligible to copy-editors, and did so with her usual sharp competence and good humor. Gregory Robbins served ably as cartographer.

The effort is dedicated with affection to Mary Layne and to Clark, Andrew, Courtney and Amy, who made room in their lives (but not too much room) for Antony and Athanasius.

Foreword

Athanasius (c. 295–373) was an Alexandrian whose life was committed at an early age to the fortunes of the Christian community there, and particularly to the theological and administrative programs of the episcopate. An advisor to Bishop Alexander, Athanasius attended the synod at Nicaea in 325, and three years later succeeded Alexander in the episcopal office. From that position he waged, for nearly a half-century, a vigorous and ultimately effective battle against his opponents within the Church—most notably Arius and his followers. The vehemence with which Athanasius advanced his cause (and resisted compromise) resulted in five periods of exile from Alexandria. He was absent from the city for more than a third of his term of office.

Athanasius's thought reveals a shift from the speculative and venturesome Alexandrian theology forged before him by Clement and Origen; it is incisive in that it succeeds in giving the keenest possible edge to the faith approved at Nicaea, and it is versatile in its manifold literary expressions.

It was during his third exile (from 355–362), after the noted monk's death in 356, that Athanasius composed the *Life of Antony*. The date of his *Letter to Marcellinus* concerning the interpretation of the Psalms cannot be fixed.

Born to an age of controversy, Athanasius thrived in it, a nemesis to his adversaries within the Church and to the Emperor Julian a "disturber of the peace and enemy of the gods." Athanasius is "the Father of Orthodoxy" to the Greek ecclesiastical tradition, and unquestionably one of the great and formidable actors on the stage of early Christian history.

Preface

To the impressive list of spiritual classics being made available by the present series, this volume adds two quite different yet fully complementary writings. Both issue, in the form of letters, from the pen of a giant among the newly favored Christians of the fourth century, Bishop Athanasius of Alexandria. The tracts are presented in a translation whose precision befits the rigor with which Athanasius dealt in all his works with Christian salvation and theology. The first letter, narrating the life of the hermit-monk Antony, has surely been the most influential writing by Athanasius, despite the cardinal importance of his doctrinal tract *On the Incarnation of the Word of God*. The other work, paling by comparison into little significance, is addressed to one Marcellinus. By explaining how to use and interpret the Psalms, Athanasius shows a side of his thought and piety seldom seen yet as important as the side shown by the biography of Antony, if we are to understand the bishop's full spirituality.

The *Life of Antony*, however dependent for literary form on the pagans' lives of their heroes, inaugurated the genre and therefore established the frame of Christian hagiography. The letter to Marcellinus, for its part, stands as the earliest extant handbook for gaining spiritually by personal, devotional meditation on, as distinct from congregational singing of, the Psalms.

PREFACE

The story of Antony quickly became the paradigm for the genre of Christian hagiography, quite as the story of Polycarp's death in Smyrna had set the style for the genre's precursor, the lives (or, better, the deaths) of the martyrs. It has been pointed out that Polycarp's story not only recorded what his admirers took to be what actually happened to him; it also, if indirectly, prescribed what were to be the main themes in the experiences of and stories about the early Christian martyrs. The ingredients I have listed (*Christianity in European History* [1979], p. 50) as "preternatural courage under trial and torment, visions foretelling the manner of death, hints of identity with Christ and of his dying in and with them [the martyrs], direct flight of the soul to heaven, and burial with veneration by fellows in the faith." Whatever individuality and personal idiosyncrasy each of the later martyrs possessed, they tended to share these traits with Polycarp and with one another. In much the same way, Antony as Athanasius's holy biographee (or hagiographee) lived out certain features of Christian salvation and sanctity that became standards for later saints, particularly monastic saints.

Now, prefaces to classical works can limit readers' profits by prescribing what they should find in the reading. Whoever reads this *Life of Antony* can well make discoveries far richer and more varied than this preface could pretend to enumerate. Therefore, we may helpfully point out a few features of the saint's experience that established patterns for later saints' experience—if they were to be real saints.

First, Antony is eminently convertible. To say "converted" might misleadingly imply some turnabout that solved once and for all a single, acute, common, spiritual problem. No so. Like the holy man in Bunyan's *Pilgrim's Progress*, who was named Christian before he entered the wicket gate, the young Antony was raised a Christian, obedient to parents and dutiful toward God (if negligent toward school). The story begins, to be sure, with a conversion, but not to Christianity—rather to the convertibility of one en route to Christian salvation. Just what Augustine and his friend Ponticianus later found so arresting in the story is exactly what Athanasius took pains to put there—Antony's convertibility to even more elevated ranges of spiritual attainment against onslaughts of the evil one.

That hints the second criterion of Christian sainthood that this book fastened on: the tradition of monastic holiness, the ladderlike quality of the saintly life, in which each higher step risked a harder fall. John Climacus (Greek *klimax*, "ladder") in the early seventh century made this point explicit, and Bernard of Clairvaux, by insisting that the steps of pride paralleled the steps of humility, drove it home. But Antony's experience implied the point plainly enough. He won a round against the devil. The devil came back reinvigorated, reinforced, ready to wage tougher battles with trickier strategies.

Third was a corollary experience, simply that spiritual exercise quickly exhausted Antony's own resources and drove him to Christ's armory for weapons and ammunition, until step-by-step increments rendered the saint for all practical purposes entirely and abjectly dependent on his Savior—indeed, to the point that the saint's identity became that of the Savior and the saint's deeds became deeds normally reserved for the work of divinity.

Fourth, having come to rely utterly on, indeed having come into an identity with, his divine Savior, the convertible saint worked good things, saving things, for others just as Christ had worked good things, saving things, for him. But, of course, no longer could one interpret Antony himself as working these benefits and this salvation, for he has

become the agent of the one with whom he was being identified through his convertibility.

Finally, without losing his personal identity as a man
named Antony, the saint yet has changed undeniably but
undefinably into, in some sense, a christ. Athanasius con-
sistently took Christian salvation to mean deification—
about the only way we can English his term *theopoiēsis* is
"deification" or "being made divine." And the evil that his
deification remedied, to be sure in a general sense sin, was
not the sin of personal guilt deserving divine punishment
but rather the sin of personal passion and finitude requir-
ing divine cure. As Antony's convertibility allowed him to
be raised by the deity above passion, his body, purged of
passion, became immaculate, and he himself became im-
mortal (at least until he died; then the testimony ceases).
Nobody after Anthanasius more boldly told of the
Christian transmutation of a mutable man or woman into
immutable deity—more precisely, immutable, deified humanity. Many have come close, precisely because Athanasius's Antony has been a criterial Christian saint, indeed,
the criterial Christian monastic saint during the long era
when the monks were the criterial Christians. To be sure,
Athanasius maintained a sharp distinction between the divine Logos as having become man in Jesus Christ and, on
the other side, the convertible Christian man or woman as
having been deified. The spirituality that Athanasius por-
trayed in Antony remained even at the end that of a man-
god, not that of a god-man. For to have become man-god,
Antony had to have been made so (*theopoiēsis*) by the god-
man. In other words, what Antony embodied in this hagiography is exactly what Irenaeus decades before had written to epitomize salvation by Jesus Christ: "He became as
we are that we might become as He is."

Did Antony, then, bring nothing of his own to the procedure? Of course, in some sense he did. He obeyed the scriptural injunction to sell all and follow the Lord. He learned from a master-hermit how to practice the discipline. He invoked the name of Christ. He recited Scripture. He knocked Satan cold by making the sign of the cross. He prayed hard and groaned mightily. He helped and taught and cured others. But in all this he was, simply, convertible—ready to be a recipient of resources and powers available to him only from or through Christ, who in turn shared entirely with the Father all the resources and powers and essence (*homoousios*) of the Godhead.

Thus the Antony of Athanasius's *Life* demonstrates in a lived life the potency of Athanasius's theology—the potency, yes; also the problematic. Already as a young man assisting his Bishop Alexander at Nicaea, Athanasius dedicated himself to a version of Christian salvation that could by definition be wrought only by the very Godhead. He found the Christology of the Arian party despicable because they commonsensically contended that all the deity that need be attributed to the divine Logos that became man in Jesus Christ was enough deity to get done the job of saving sinful men and women. The salvation experienced by the Arians was a salvation they shared with a Savior who had, to put it bluntly, "made it." By participating in the Savior's success, they themselves made it. Their salvation was eminently workable. It invoked no such unthinkables as that of a son identical in essence with his father.

But to Athanasius, as demonstrated in his story of Antony, the Arians' salvation fell short of conveying what human creatures most needed: namely, the vanquishing of the hallmark of their creatureliness—finitude or death. Were the savior a finite creature, however otherwise divine, the saved would still die. To be sure, this insistence on the highest conceivable, perhaps inconceivable, Christology raised two grave problems. If salvation were to a state quite beyond creatureliness, no creature could do one whit about or toward being saved. Moreover, if the savior required for this salvation were utterly uncreaturely, he could hardly have "become as we are in order that we might become as He is." While Athanasius, despite the Arians' and the semi-Arians' arguments, never owned up to these problems in his version of salvation and Christology, in fact at least once he tried to cover them. Therefore, the selection of *A Letter of Athanasius . . . to Marcellinus on the Interpretation of the Psalms* as companion-piece to the *Life of Antony* in this volume is, in this light, quite ingenious.

By Athanasius's time the memorization of the Psalms by many Christians and their habitual use as songs in worship by all Christians we know about were matters of long-standing tradition. The tradition had hardly been challenged except for the mid-second-century protest against the Old Testament by Marcion and his followers. The great catechetical school at Athanasius's own city of Alexandria had, from the mid-second century with Pantaenus through the mid-third century with Origen, perfected a special method for interpreting Scriptures, particularly the Old Testament and especially the Psalms. This method allowed biblical passages that said nothing directly about the figure of Christ to yield the clearest and most illuminating insights into that figure. Medieval scholastics who perfected this method boiled it down to a slogan about the four "senses" or "meanings" of any passage: The literal teaches you facts, the allegorical what you should believe, the moral what you should do, and the anagogical where you are headed. Of these, the literal was least important, for virtually any "facts" could be made to point allegorically to

Christ as the standard of Christian belief and action and hope.

In writing about the use of the Psalms in personal Christian devotion, Athanasius was thus able to say much about salvation in Christ without having to say much of anything either historical or theological about Christ. Harp as elsewhere he usually did on the one string of Nicene "orthodoxy" against the Arians, here he struck another melody. Instead of debating an already incarnate Christ and already accomplished salvation, this song foretold a coming Savior.

The Psalms, on this construction, summarized the entire Old Testament as those books anticipated and prepared for the New Testament. The readying of Israel for the Savior became allegorically the readying of the human soul for salvation. In the letter Athanasius praises the Book of Psalms thus: "For in addition to the other things in which it enjoys an affinity and fellowship with the other books, it possesses, beyond that, this marvel of its own—namely, that it contains even the emotions of each soul, and it has the changes and rectifications of these delineated and regulated in itself" (§10). To be sure, "grace is from the Savior" (no. 13). Yet "the Book of Psalms possesses somehow the perfect image for the souls' course of life" (no. 14). Then, in perspicuous detail, Athanasius enumerates the emotional states and the crises and the temptations and the rejoicings of daily life, finding for whatever occasion apt psalms to soothe the disturbed affections into passionless.

By using this inexhaustible and universal pharmacopoeia of what we might call "psalm-balm," the person who wanted to deepen his spiritual life could in fact do very important things toward his own salvation. In preparation for conversion by the Savior, the soul in imitation of Israel as epitomized by the Psalms could indeed "make it" toward salvation from a Savior who in the process of expectation by Israel and then of incarnation had in some sense "made it."

In a word, by approaching salvation and Christology through the historical career of God's chosen people, then by allegorizing this history into the inner or emotional life of the individual soul of a Christian expecting salvation, Athanasius covered the major problems of his metaphysical soteriology and Christology. On this reading, the Savior did indeed "become as we are in order that we might become as He is." For both these movements, both "His" becoming and "our" becoming, are now made into processes involving desire, intention, work, and attainment. And Athanasius needed to add not one iota to qualify the Nicene identity (*homoousios*) of the saving Logos with the Father in the Godhead. If his technical theology had made salvation so absolute that the Savior was remote and the saved paralyzed from personal achievement through devotion, this plan of personal devotion involved an accessible Savior approachable through meditation on the soul's preparation for salvation. Like East and West, this theology and this piety never quite met. But his piety did find expression by the master of this theology.

And what can all this ancient spirituality mean for moderns? The answer can be brief. Certainly all this is utterly foreign to our mode of being in the world. There is no way for us to parlay supposed similarities with Antony into an empathetic act of crawling into his skin. But we do imaginatively construct the universes in which we move and live, and by the willing suspension of disbelief (itself far removed from traditional Christian believing) we enter, for a time, into those universes. Precisely *because* the universe of Athanasius and of the Antony about whom he wrote and of the Marcellinus to whom he wrote is different from "our own" universe (whatever that may be), we can imaginatively reconstruct theirs and enter it, for a time. To do so is not by any means to gain their blessings (whatever they may have been), any more than it is to suffer their diseases or to believe their superstitions. We cannot become then, nor even vicariously "have" their experiences. What we can do is to stretch ourselves by trying on imaginatively for a time the way things were for them. Certainly by doing so we gain magnanimity; literally, we enlarge our souls or minds.

There may be modern readers of these works by Athanasius who want more, who yearn to acquire the Christian salvation or apotheosis or *theopoēsis* that was theirs. Such readers, if any, would do well to heed the main line of Athanasius's theology, to the effect that one can do absolutely nothing to avail such salvation, but only wait to see if it might perchance befall. Otherwise, such readers, if any, must adopt the strange allegorical method of gaining balms from the Psalms.

Whatever the hope of reward from reading these works, the reader may be confident that the translations here provided transfer Athanasius's Greek into our English with the minimum of addition or remainder in meaning. The bishop won his skills of debate in battle, and it seems safe to assume that he wrote what he meant as precisely as he could. Professor Gregg quite rightly cleaves to the text, providing as close an English equivalent to each word and phrase as will remain readable. Judged by very high standards of English style, an infelicity is here or there to be found. But felicities of one language often beget distortions of the other. The translator's fidelity to these texts ensures that the reader receives in these works Athanasius's meaning, so far as feasible in the order of his thoughts and in the equivalence of his words.

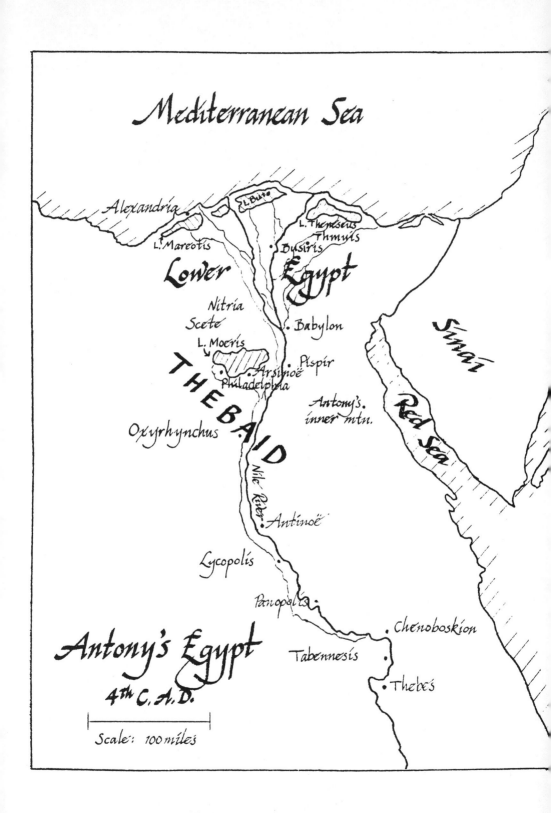

Mediterranean Sea

Alexandria

L. Buto

L. Mareotis

L. Thennesis
Thmuis

Busiris

Lower

Egypt

Nitria

Scete

Babylon

L. Moeris

Pispir

Arsinoë
Philadelphia

THEBAID

Antony's
inner mtn.

Oxyrhynchus

Sinai

Red Sea

Nile River

Antinoë

Lycopolis

Panopolis

Chenoboskion

Antony's Egypt
4th C. A. D.

Tabennesis

Thebes

Scale: 100 miles

Introduction

The two early Christian writings brought together in this volume differ considerably in subject and in form. One employs narrative to set forth the career and teachings of a celebrated "man of God," while the other offers fairly systematic instruction concerning the nature and use of the Psalter. Despite their contrasting purposes and styles, these two lengthy epistles bear the common stamp of Christianity in the patristic age, and readers will soon sense that both works are informed by assumptions, concepts, and energies that are as fundamental to the era of the church fathers as they seem foreign to our own.

Although the authorship of the *Life of Antony* has been a matter of debate,[1] both of these treatises are now widely thought to be products of Athanasius, the controversial and frequently exiled bishop of Alexandria during the tumultuous years from 328 to 373.[2] Advocacy of the Christian beliefs articulated at the Council of Nicaea in 325 (called thereafter "orthodoxy" by its champions) was Athanasius's consuming vocation, and it was in his capacity as antiheretical activist and writer that he became one of the most vivid and forceful personalities in fourth-century ecclesiastical and political affairs. Although the works published here do not purport to be polemical writings, they too provide evidence of Athanasius's vigilance against unorthodox ideas and doctrines.

1

INTRODUCTION

By the standards of the classical world, the *Life of Antony* was an immediate literary sensation. It enjoyed broad circulation among literate members of the Church, presumably was read to others, and quickly was made available in translation to those who did not read Greek. The treatise contained a view of Christian living too revolutionary in its implications for individuals and institutions to be labeled, in the modern sense, "devotional reading." An encounter with the *Vita Antonii* could have traumatic effect. We may take it for granted that Athanasius's account of the deeds and powers of Antony appealed also to readers beyond the Christian community, for though the taste for stories about the exploits of holy men and women is present in most cultures and times, this appetite was especially strong in late Roman society. To our age and culture the figure of Antony is thoroughly startling—even offensive. Other centuries did not think him so bizarre, but from the first there must have been a mixture of admiration and puzzled fascination in the responses of those, Christians and non-Christians alike, who learned of his life.

The *Letter to Marcellinus* created no comparable stir. Athanasius's treatment of the Book of Psalms is provocative in ways quite distinct from the story of Antony, and its subject is, in the strict sense, more esoteric: It contains information and direction intended exclusively for those who make use of the Psalter in their public and private prayer, and do so as Christians.

THE LIFE OF ANTONY

The Simplicity and Complexity of a Classic

It was apparently quite soon after Antony's death in 356 that Athanasius answered a request for more informa-

INTRODUCTION

tion about the renowned Egyptian's life.³ His correspondents wanted to know of Antony's youth, of his beginning in *askēsis* (discipline), and of the manner in which he died. Athanasius hurriedly pieced together a narrative that was destined to become one of the most influential writings in Christian history. It told of Antony's early years, the decision to disengage himself from the pressures and obligations of conventional society,⁴ the trials endured and the contests won as his pursuit of virtue led him deeper into the desert, his instruction to other Christian solitaries, his dealings with visitors to his cell and his own dramatic visits to Alexandria in times of crisis, and, finally, his carefully considered death and burial.

Within a few decades the *Life of Antony* had won acclaim not only among Greek-speaking Christians in the eastern Mediterranean, but also among Latin Christians in Gaul and Italy. A modern scholar remarks that "by 400 [Antony] was already a hero of the past."⁵ This was largely due to Athanasius, whose presentation of the monk's career was quickly attaining the status of a classic.

What was its appeal? It is doubtful that any single answer will suffice. Research over the last century has revealed Athanasius's *Vita Antonii* to be a work of multiple dimensions and considerable literary ingenuity. Like the rich and stylized Coptic tapestries of the period, this striking portrait of Antony is artfully simple; the selection of materials and the placing of highlights show Athanasius to be sensitive to a range of tastes. So it is very likely that the *Life of Antony* was differently attractive to different readers. If we seek a common denominator in its popularity, it may be possible to point to the successful combination of two indispensable elements in any good tale, and particularly in a classical romance: the *Vita Antonii* featured a larger-than-life central character, and a strange and exotic setting for his exploits. For every reader, the monk was an arresting figure as he fought demons in a tomb, or performed miracles, or experienced visions of his future, or confounded sages who sought to embarrass him. Perhaps it is also true that in varying degrees the entire audience for which Athanasius wrote was preoccupied with two energies that seem to intersect in Antony, for his story can be read as the interplay of unflinching self-interrogation and self-exertion, on the one hand, and help, on the other—help in the form of heaven-sent power. Warfare with the demons is at the same time warfare with the self, and this contest has meaning only as it results in the attainment of divine empowerment and favor. Antony's wrestlings and hopes must have been shared by many.[6]

The unresolved and still haunting question about the *Life of Antony* has to do with what kind of classic it is. Judgments about its controlling theme and its literary format cover a vast field. A number of suggestions have been advanced by those scholars intent on underlining the connection between the *Vita Antonii* and certain "classic" biblical themes and motifs. It is argued that: the basic structure of the work derives from the temptation story in the Gospels; the life of simplicity that Antony embraces is traceable to the earliest days of the Christian community (depicted in Acts 2:42ff.); the paradigm for this "man of God" is provided by the tradition of the Old Testament prophets, the apostles, the martyrs, and the angels.[7] These interpretations of the structure and dominant interests of the *Life of Antony* are of a piece with a broader claim voiced by Louis Bouyer, who finds "nothing more purely Christian than the antecedents of monasticism, and nothing more purely evangelical than its primary motivations."[8]

Such adamant defenses of the biblical and Christian basis for the *Life of Antony* stand as responses to a series of

4

studies dating from the early decades of this century in which sources for Athanasius's work were found in classical literature. Evidence was marshaled to indicate Athanasius's familiarity with and dependence on such works as the *Life of Pythagoras*, Philostratus's *Life of Apollinius of Tyana*, Porphyry's *Life of Plotinus*, and the *Life of King Agesilaus* by Xenophon.[9] The identification of parallels in these works and in segments of the *Vita Antonii* have not been judged equally convincing, but the cumulative effect of this body of scholarship has been to establish Athanasius's willingness to employ as a model for his treatment of Antony some features of the classical genre that treats the life of the hero or the sage.[10]

Is the *Life of Antony* a classic in that it catches up great biblical and Christian themes such as temptation in the wilderness and the *imitatio Christi*, or is it classic in quite another sense, in that it conforms to the prescription of a Greco-Roman *encomium*, which relates the nationality, training, and deeds of a celebrated personage who has died?[11] There is no reason to pose these as mutually exclusive options. Athanasius, like other patristic writers (and unlike some moderns who have attempted to make biblical and Greek conception and perspective strictly antithetical) did not utterly abandon classical literature and learning out of enthusiasm for the Christian faith. In this connection, Athanasius's reason for writing the *Life of Antony* bears close scrutiny. He sends a double message, suggesting at the work's beginning that Antony's story is meant to provide an example for other monks, but adding at the end of the treatise that the *Vita* might profitably be read to pagans as well. In composing the narrative, Athanasius has in mind both Christian readers who might draw inspiration from it and those potential converts to whom he had addressed other works *(Contra Gentes* and *De Incarnatione)*—

INTRODUCTION

indeed, Antony's encounters with visiting philosophers echo some of Athanasius's favorite apologetic themes.[12]

The *Life of Antony* is, then, a classic of several kinds, intended for readers of more than one type. Someone steeped in the literature and philosophy of late antique culture (pagan or Christian) would have recognized in Antony the profile of the *sophos*, or wise man, and would have taken careful note of a new casting of the ancient Greek ideal of self-sufficiency in Athanasius's portrait. For Christian readers, Antony not only dramatized the Gospel's call to absolute obedience, he represented an issue at the heart of the Christian proclamation—the danger, as Paul put it, of being "conformed to this world" (Rom. 12:2). Seen in that light, the career of Antony, the "man of God," confronted the Church and its members with a radical definition of Christian identity and purpose. The man on the boundary appealed to many in the center. He came to symbolize, through Athanasius's artistry, "the type of the Christian, the ideal portrait of the human being, as he should be."[13]

Antony's Discipline: The Shape of Spirituality

Through the centuries the most persistent and sharply focused interest in the *Life of Antony* has been found among those either in the ascetic tradition or concerned with patterns and developments in Christian spiritual life. In the process of telling Antony's story, Athanasius shed valuable light on those practices and values that constitute *askēsis*, the austere and rigorous discipline undertaken by monks and hermits in the third century. Whether later monastic practice took the form of solitary isolation or communal separation from the world, and whether its expressions were harsh and dramatic (as in the case of the "pillar saints" in Syria) or moderate and learned (as in the case of

6

INTRODUCTION

the Cappadocian Fathers of the fourth century), the behavior and pursuits of the ascetic set the terms for the Church's ideal of the life of devotion. Where the monk's austerities could not be imitated, they could be admired. And ordinary people of the Christian community were always imaginative enough to participate vicariously in the trials and triumphs of these heroic figures who underwent a new kind of martyrdom, martyrdom of the conscience (chap. 47). Much consideration has been given, therefore, to the prominent features of Antony's regimen, since they have become integral elements in the definition of ascetic piety—for example, the importance of work in the monk's discipline (in this case, the labor of weaving, chap. 53), the role of Scripture in prayer and exorcism (chaps. 9, 13, 39–40), the practices of fasting and sleeping on the ground (chap. 7), simple—even harsh—dress, and disregard for certain bodily needs and pleasures (chap. 47).

Two aspects of Antony's discipline have drawn particular notice. More than in a source like the *Sayings of the Fathers*, the *Life of Antony* accentuates demonology. Athanasius's portrait of the monk's career suggests that the desert life is as much warfare as serenity and solitude. The desolate places are crowded with Satan's forces, who are disturbers of the peace. And as is the case in other early monastic sources, the portrayal of demons in the *Vita Antonii* is subtle and psychologically suggestive. These threatening beings are capable of manifesting themselves in the guises of just those temptations to which individual monks are most susceptible (chap. 42). Self-scrutiny is thus an essential and continuing part of progress in virtue. "The demonic stood not merely for all that was hostile *to* man; the demons summed up all that was anomalous and incomplete *in* man."[14] Yet Athanasius's Antony is depicted as one who gained mastery over Satan and his agents. As a person whose only allegiance is owed to Christ, Antony is capable of frustrating the stratagems of his foes. So he tutors the other monks in the use of prayer and the sign of the cross for the dispersion of evil spirits, and gives detailed advice about how to determine whether one's cell is being visited by demons or by angels (chaps. 39–43, 88). It is this emphasis on the monk's vocation as warrior against demons that modern apologists for asceticism stress in answer to the charge that the monk is an escapist. The monk's retirement from the world is, at the very least, an ambiguous retreat, for though he separates himself from the distractions and nagging pressures of ordinary human community, Athanasius labors to inform the reader that the wilderness to which Antony flees holds more significant challenges and dangers. When Antony finds no relief from an enthusiastic crowd during a rare visit to the city, he assures those around him that he must contend with equal numbers—of demons—at his cell in the wilderness (chap. 70).

Our reference to the monk's retirement from society brings us to the second aspect of the *Vita Antonii* that has been the subject of much discussion and debate. It is no longer claimed (as it sometimes was) that Antony was the first person whose Christian aspirations caused him to take up the life of a separatist, an anchorite (from the Greek word *anachōrein*, "to withdraw, to leave"). There is evidence within the treatise itself of holy men living as solitaries on the fringes of villages; it was from them that the young Antony learned his first skills in the discipline. The more frequent (and more important) assertion is that Antony's distinctive contribution to the development of asceticism was his transfer of the monastic life from the periphery of established communities to the barren and isolated setting of a hermitage, and indeed Athanasius remarks that before him "no monk knew at all the great desert" (chap.

3). There is no reason to doubt Antony's reputation as such a pioneer, nor to doubt that this marked a new epoch in Christian experience. It is the nature of this isolated existence, however, that bears closer examination. The *Life of Antony* conveys the strong impression that, far from being removed from society after being led to his refuge in the "inner mountain" near the Red Sea, Antony is significantly involved with people and their affairs. He is subject to a constant stream of visitors, each of whom seeks something from him. There are hints of some protocol or clearance procedure for gaining an audience, and we note repeatedly the presence of interpreters (chaps. 58, 84, 72). Although we are told that Antony has distanced himself from populated areas, he is far from *incommunicado*—he seems more accessible than ever. Antony the holy man is becoming himself the destination for pilgrims and for those in need of a healer and wonder-worker. The monk's isolation has more geographical than social reality, for (as research by Peter Brown has shown) by the fourth century the holy man is emerging as a figure of real importance to the economic and political equilibrium of the culture from which he has separated himself; his role as mediator and arbiter (chap. 84) depends on and is legitimized by his disinterest and independence, but particularly by his demonstrated power.[15]

One of the many conclusions that might be drawn from this revised estimate of Antony's life as hermit is that the monk's "spirituality," like the role accorded him in society, has been much too narrowly defined. It is at least arguable that the full range of Antony's actions in the *Vita* need to be regarded as components of his spiritual life, since every episode is presented as part of his advance in sanctity. At any rate, Athanasius does nothing to suggest that Antony's prayerful contests with demons are more distinctly spiritual or have a more hallowing effect than his debates with Greek philosophers, his denunciations of schismatics and heretics, or his endeavors as "charismatic *Ombudsman* in a tension-ridden countryside."[16]

A final comment should be added to this set of remarks about Antony's spirituality. The monk's simplicity of knowledge is repeatedly emphasized in the narrative, even while he silences sages in debate and delivers himself of cogent theological statements. The reader is not expected to miss the point. Though Antony is not armed with syllogisms and the fruits of a classical education, his grasp of Christian fundamentals and his stark reasoning, utterly lacking in ornament, reveal his durable and holy wisdom. The stress on Antony's lack of learning is connected with an assumption about the health of the psyche that is articulated more than once: The monk's training serves to return the soul to its original and natural state. It is clear faith and plain reasoning, rather than facility in speech and argument, that aid this process. But there is in Antony's lack of sophistication and culture another message. He signals a mode of Christian achievement, an opportunity to join an elite that bars no one on the basis of social pedigree, lack of official sponsorship, or privileged training. Initially a movement that attracted lay persons rather than those in orders, asceticism (like martyrdom before it) opened opportunity for Christian vocation and celebrity to many who had never enjoyed elevated status in their communities. Ironically, the figure who typified dissociation from society was also, for some, a symbol of social advancement. Had not Antony risen from obscure (though not impoverished) origins to become the ally of bishops, the counselor of emperors? We may assume that most of the persons drawn to this new form of Christian discipleship sought more enduring goals than increased prestige, but the idea of recompense was by no means foreign to the ascetic ideal. Despite reminders throughout the *Life of Antony* that the monk exercised a power not his own, and suffered no distress when his prayers went unanswered, the biography reveals a pervasive and intense interest in the effects of the disciplined life.[17] Antony's domination of the demons and his numerous healings and visions are presented unambiguously as results of his zeal and rigor. The spiritual labors of the ascetic may have been in some sense their own reward, but they clearly were not the only expected reward.

Antony in the Arian Controversy

It has long been recognized that the portrait of Antony as an outspoken adversary of the Arians, whether or not it has a sound historical basis, is deeply colored by his biographer's passionate advocacy of the doctrine of Nicaea. When anathematizing heretics in the *Vita Antonii*, Antony is speaking the words of the bishop of Alexandria.[18] The degree of Antony's actual knowledge of and involvement in the dispute is, under the circumstances, difficult to determine, especially in view of the fact that the teachings attributed to Antony in documents like the *Sayings of the Fathers* give no evidence of his interest in the issues that occupied polemical theologians and churchmen like Athanasius and Arius.[19]

It is worth asking how integral to Athanasius's purpose in writing the *Life of Antony* was the desire to align the celebrated (and recently deceased) monk firmly with the orthodox partisans in the controversy. As we know from Athanasius's correspondence, followers of Arius were, in the late 350s, bidding for the support of Egyptian monastics, and the *Vita* itself preserves notice of the Arian contention that he shared their doctrine.[20] To what extent did Athanasius strive to accentuate and elaborate Antony's character as an exemplar of orthodox piety?

On three occasions, Athanasius's Antony explicitly condemns the Arians and their dangerous teaching (chaps. 68–70, 89, 91). But there is reason to believe that the anti-Arian purposes in the biography are not confined to those episodes. Issues central to the battle with the Arians seem also to have determined the manner in which Athanasius depicted Antony's various achievements. The monk's actions and his daily advance in holiness had to be shown to stem directly from the power and grace sent by Christ, the fully divine and co-essential Son of God. Athanasius maintained (with Nicaea) that the salvation and sanctification of mortal creatures depended entirely on the power of the Son of God. The guarantee of the Son's power and of his capacity to save humankind was the substance *(ousia)* he shared with the Father. According to orthodox soteriology, God's *natural* Son extended saving assistance *(boētheia)* to those who would become his *adopted* sons and daughters.[21]

Arius and his allies held an altogether different view of the Savior and the means of human salvation: As Christ the creature had been chosen and named "Son" on account of works he performed (works foreknown by God), so also Christian believers, following the example of his consistent obedience, might attain the status of God's sons and daughters. Fully aware of this Arian teaching, Athanasius took pains to demonstrate that Antony's discipline and his advance in virtue were controlled by orthodoxy's understanding of salvation. It is this concern that stands behind the persistent editorial reminders that Antony's victories over demons and his miraculous healings were not his own accomplishments, but works of Christ (chaps. 5, 7, 48, 58). Similarly, the dramatic intervention of a descending beam of light that rescues the entombed Antony from demonic

Athanasius vs Arians

assault (chap. 10) bears the clear stamp of Athanasius's Nicene Christology—the help and deliverance of creatures can derive only from the Son's divine brilliance.[22] The portrait of Antony and his exploits is painstakingly drawn. By insisting that the holy man's virtue and power are bestowed by Christ (and only in a qualified sense *achieved*), Athanasius protects Antony from an *askēsis* consonant with the Arian view—a pursuit of virtue common both to Christ and to his fellow creatures in which sonship and sanctification are won through moral advance, through the steady choice of the good.

It is yet another measure of the complexity and subtlety of Athanasius's portrait of the desert saint that Antony, in addition to his other aspects, becomes a vehicle for the doctrinal commitments of the author. One of the chief purposes of the work was to counteract, by painting Antony in strong orthodox hues, the Arians' effort to gain support for their cause from among the ranks of the ascetics.

The Antonian Tradition

Though other traditions about Antony (e.g., in Palladius's *Lausiac History* and in Jerome's account of the hermit Paul) complemented its effect, Athanasius's idealized and forceful biography of Antony was clearly the chief impetus for the monk's broad popularity and continuing influence. It was not only during the formative decades of the Christian monastic movement that the *Vita Antonii* had its impact. The testings and miracles of Antony fixed themselves in the consciousness of the Church and of Western culture as a sharp image of what a life committed to God demands and promises. History does not record all of the transformations of individual and institutional lives in which the figure and example of Antony played a part. There were surely many, unnamed and unknown to us, who saw in Antony's perseverance a plumb line condemning their shallowness of conviction, and who answered the summons to a more stringent Christian allegiance. No more than a few of the notices of the rich and extensive Antonian tradition can be mentioned here.

In the fifty years after the composition of the *Vita* several writers mentioned Athanasius's work with appreciation. Gregory of Nazianzus describes it as a monastic rule cast in narrative, and Palladius indicates his dependence on Athanasius for a story he relates about Antony.[23] The anonymous author of the *Life of Pachomius*, in the course of describing the cooperative relationship that existed between his hero and Antony, reports that in the *Vita* Athanasius "drew on informed monastic sources and wrote with accuracy."[24] We have evidence of enthusiasm for circulating the *Life of Antony* in remarks of Jerome (347–420), who tells of his familiarity with a Greek text (which he attributes to Athanasius) as well as a Latin translation prepared by Evagrius of Antioch.[25] Another Latin text, cruder and less paraphrastic than that which bears Evagrius's name, indicates the existence of at least two Latin versions of the *Vita* by the end of the fourth century.[26]

Augustine of Hippo (354–430) gives no indication in his *Confessions* which Latin text of the *Life of Antony* is known to his circle of friends. What he does tell us, however, is of immense interest. It is a graphic account of the impact Antony's story had on a particular kind of person in late Roman society—someone whose personal and professional identity had become ripe for change and redirection. While visiting his friend Augustine, Ponticianus relates an experience of one of his acquaintances in Trêves. This young man was moved to such shame and such love of holiness by reading the *Life of Antony* (which a Christian gave him while he strolled with a companion) that he promptly abandoned his career as a special agent of the emperor, canceled his wedding plans, and was converted—to the ascetic life. It was, Ponticianus says, a case of his "mind . . . being divested of the world," his heart "fixed upon heaven."[27] Ponticianus's tale contributes to the building agitation of Augustine, who, remembering Antony's sense of being directly and personally addressed by the recitation of the Gospel in his village church, heeds the child's voice that comes into his Milanese garden and rushes at last to embrace orthodox Christianity in the only form that can satisfy him—asceticism.

The starker anchorite ideal personified in Antony was not to dominate monasticism as it took hold throughout the Christianized world. It was the model of communal or cenobite (from *koinos bios*, "common life") asceticism associated with Antony's Egyptian contemporary Pachomius (286–346) that won the important endorsement of Basil, Bishop of Caesarea (330–379). This organization of monks and monasteries under a superior was reflected in the institutions that were to prove so decisive to the Church's future in Byzantium and in Western Europe—most notably in the community founded by Benedict at Monte Cassino in 529. The success of the Pachomian monastic scheme did not diminish the popularity of Antony, who epitomized the solitary discipline. Much of what he stood for could be incorporated into the communal life, and beyond that, the *Vita* (as read by people in the fourth and fifth centuries) probably did not give so definite an impression of Antony as a recluse, since the work abounds with traces of the conferences he held with monks who looked on him as a father. It is also clear that the prevalence of monastic federations did not by any means eliminate the phenomenon of the individual ascetic virtuoso. As much a part of the story of the westward spread of monasticism as the establishments connected with the names of Martin of Tours and John Cassian are the countless hermits who pursued God in isolation, and never failed to fascinate the general public. (It was publicity from Benedict's austere routine in a cave that produced his first disciples.) And to the style of ascetic life that came to flourish among the Celts in the sixth century, Antony's rigor and self-deprivation could not have been intimidating.

In the lore surrounding the Egyptian desert fathers that was transmitted throughout Medieval and Byzantine churches, the name of Antony retained its luster: He was Egypt's most famous example of the quest for individual perfection and of the power given to those submissive to the "bloodless martyrdom." The Antonian ideal formed a central part of the bold definition of holy living that won converts to Christianity. It was at the same time a reminder to ecclesiastical officials and laity alike of the Church's ambiguous and dangerous relation to the affairs of the world.

Antony, the subject of Athanasius's masterpiece, endured. In *The Love of Learning and the Desire for God*, Dom Leclercq explains why:

> He remained truly the Father of all monks; and so in all milieus and in every period of the Western Middle Ages they considered themselves as truly his sons. Everywhere they claimed his support, sometimes even against each other. During each monastic revival, they hark back to ancient Egypt; they want, they say, to revive Egypt, to inaugurate a new Egypt and they call upon St. Anthony, his example and his writings.... St. Anthony represents for all, an ideal whose essential characteristic is its potential for realization in different ways. St. Anthony's life, then, for the medieval

monks is not simply an historical text, a source of information about a definitely dead past. It is a living text, a means
of formation of a monastic life.[28]

The popularity Antony enjoyed through centuries of
art necessitates a final comment about the vitality of the
Antonian tradition. Iconographical studies of Antony reveal a variety of works, widely dispersed, from the fourth
through the twelfth centuries. The monk is featured in ter-
ra cotta ampullas, stone crosses, frescoes, sculpted portals
and capitals in churches, manuscript illustrations, and mo-
saics.[29] Some index of his popularity is reflected in the sur-
vival of more than two hundred representations (paintings
and frescoes) from the fourteenth century alone. Along
with the legend (from Jerome) of Antony's visit to the cell
of Paul the hermit, the theme of Antony's contests with demons was favored by artists. Antony is customarily depicted as besieged by fantastic beasts (he is either in a posture
of distress or oblivious to their assault) or confronted by an
alluring woman (who frequently sports telltale horns or
hooves).[30] Perhaps the best known of these works are the
temptation scenes by Bosch, Huys, Tintoretto, and Grüne-
wald (the Isenheim altarpiece), all of which were produced
in the sixteenth century. An effective treatment of the
theme was painted by Max Ernst in 1945.

Major Works of Athanasius

Born sometime around 295, Athanasius spent the major portion of his life as an official, thinker, and pastor in
the Church. From 319 (when he was ordained deacon and
became an assistant to Bishop Alexander) until his death in
373, Athanasius was involved in ecclesiastical affairs both
in Alexandria and throughout the empire. By their range

and volume his writings testify to Athanasius's energy and to his fine talent for bringing to sharp expression those propositions most crucial to his understanding of the Christian faith. Athanasius had the temperament and mind required by an age in which advocates of Christianity had to possess needed skills of attack and defense—as much for their altercations with other Christians as for their encounters with pagan theologians and critics.

The most elaborate (and influential) of Athanasius's apologetic writings is the double volume entitled *Against the Pagans* and *On the Incarnation of the Word*, in which both traditional and distinctively Athanasian arguments are presented to support claims of the superiority of Christianity to pagan piety. Apologies of a different sort include three defenses of Athanasius's actions during the Arian controversy: *Apology against the Arians, Apology to the Emperor Constantius*, and *Apology for his Flight* (all written in the 350s). A lengthy letter, now called *History of the Arians*, also belongs to this class of writings.

The majority of Athanasius's doctrinal writing was devoted to combating the ideas of Arius (256–336) and his followers. Chief among these are the three *Orations against the Arians* (the fourth *Oration* is inauthentic), *Defense of the Nicene Council (De Decretis), On the Councils of Ariminum and Seleucia (De Synodis)*, and a number of letters, including the *Encyclical Epistle to the Bishops*, the *Encyclical Epistle to the Bishops of Egypt and Libya*, and the *Epistle to the African Bishops*. Athanasius's *Letters concerning the Holy Spirit (Ad Serapionem)* address the question of the divinity of the third person of the Trinity (an issue that emerged in the later stages of the Arian dispute), and the important *Synodal Letter to the Antiochenes* reflects the state of the controversy in 362. The *Letter to Epictetus* and the *Letter to Adelphius* signal the emergence of new questions about the nature of Christ that would be debated among Christians even after the Council of Chalcedon in 451.

The *Life of Antony* is characteristically classified as an ascetical treatise or a hagiography. It is generally conceded to be Athanasius's most influential writing.

Athanasius's biblical commentaries are known to us only in fragments that preserve traces of his books on the Psalms, Ecclesiastes, the Song of Songs, and Genesis. The *Letter to Marcellinus* is the only surviving complete Athanasian work dealing exclusively with Scripture and its interpretation.

A valuable portion of Athanasius's correspondence is comprised of *Festal Letters*, letters customarily sent to churches in the Alexandrian bishop's charge to announce the date of Easter, to inform believers of events affecting the Church, and to encourage proper seasonal observances. Thirteen of these epistles (written between 329 and 348) are extant in Syriac versions, and provide informative glimpses of Athanasius's style as bishop and pastor.

Translating the Life of Antony

The Greek text that is the basis for this translation is found in Migne's *Patrologia Graeca* 26 (1887), columns 835–976. The Migne text itself was taken over from the Benedictine edition prepared in 1698 by Bernard De Montfaucon.

Of the several modern translations of the treatise that exist, the following have been consulted:

English

Ellershaw, H., trans. *Life of Antony*, in *Select Writings and Letters of Athanasius, Bishop of Alexandria*, ed. by A.

Robertson. A Select Library of Nicene and Post-Nicene Fathers of the Christian Church, Second Series 4. New York: The Christian Literature Company, 1892, pp. 195–221 (Reprinted by Wm. B. Eerdmans of Grand Rapids, Michigan in 1957).

McLaughlin, Dom J. B. *St. Antony the Hermit, By St. Athanasius.* New York: Benziger Brothers, 1924.

Meyer, R. T. *St. Athanasius, The Life of Saint Antony.* Ancient Christian Writers 10. Westminster, Md.: The Newman Press, 1950.

German

Richard, P. A. *Des heiligen Athanasius Leben des Antonius*, in *Des heiligen Athanasius ausgewählte Schriften* 2. Bibliothek der Kirchenväter. Kempten: Jos. Kösel'schen Buchhandlung, 1875, pp. 215–330.

Among the translation decisions I have made, one in particular should be mentioned. The word *askēsis* has, in nearly all instances, been rendered as "discipline" (rather than "asceticism"). Although it is clear that Athanasius is moving toward a technical sense of what "the discipline" (or, as it might have been translated, "the practice") entails, it seems preferable to use the simpler and less historically freighted "discipline" in order that the treatise itself might be allowed to give content and context to the term.

New Testament quotations are given in the translation of the Revised Standard Version (RSV). Old Testament citations reflect the book titles and divisions as well as the Psalm numeration of the Greek text—the Septuagint (LXX) that Athanasius used—rather than the Hebrew text—for example, 4 Kings 19:35 is equivalent to 2 Kings 19:35 in English translations of the Hebrew text, and

Psalm 38:14 is equivalent to Psalm 39:14 in the RSV translation. (The LXX reflects this difference of one digit from
Psalm 10 through Psalm 146.) Translations of Old Testament passages are adapted from: L. C. L. Brenton trans.,
The Septuagint Version of the Old Testament and Apocrypha
(Grand Rapids, Mich.: Zondervan Publishing House,
1972).

THE LETTER TO MARCELLINUS

A Pastoral Epistle

In at least one respect, this Athanasian writing is an
unlikely companion piece for the renowned *Life of Antony.*
The *Letter to Marcellinus* has not sparked modern scholarly
debate, and there is no evidence, beyond the fact of its sur-
vival, that it enjoyed unusual fame when it appeared. It has
in common with the *Vita* the form of an occasional letter—
once again, an answer to a request for information and edi-
fication. Though Athanasius did not, in all likelihood, expect his epistles to be seen or heard only by their recipi-
ents, there is less explicit consciousness of a wider
readership in this document. The result is a letter that im-
presses the reader as being conventional—certainly less
dramatic and evocative than the story of Antony. And
though its subject is a matter of general interest and useful-
ness, it seems to have been a directed pastoral communica-
tion.

During an illness, Marcellinus (a deacon in the Alexandrian church?)[31] has busied himself in the study of the
Bible, and has set for himself the ambitious goal of learning
"the meaning contained in each psalm" (chap. 1). It is evident from the design and content of Athanasius's response
that he does not consider his friend's project preposterous.

INTRODUCTION

We may be correct in assuming that such an endeavor could only have been the occupation of clergy and ascetics (reference is made to Marcellinus's "discipline"), whose daily routines must have afforded more opportunity for concentrated consideration of Scripture. But an exchange of letters with this expressed purpose cannot have been born in a vacuum; the spiritual needs and practices of church leaders cannot have been entirely divorced from those of ordinary Christians. The topic that prompts the letters alerts us to the importance of the Psalter to people throughout the early Christian community. Marcellinus and Athanasius continue an enterprise that had its beginnings in the New Testament writings themselves: the use of the Psalms in the articulation of Christian belief and self-understanding.

By the fourth century, Christian thinkers had devised several distinct ways of putting questions to a psalm text. There were levels of meaning to be discerned and distinguished, and the city of Alexandria was famous for an erudite approach to Scripture that promised to lead a receptive student from simpler to more divine interpretations. Or a biblical text (e.g., one from a psalm) could be examined and then employed as a weapon in a doctrinal dispute. So Athanasius had insisted against the Arians that the line "In your light we shall see light" (LXX: Ps. 35:10) argued for the eternality of the Son of God.[32]

In his *Letter to Marcellinus* Athanasius alludes to allegorical possibilities and to the doctrinal implications of certain passages in the Psalms, but these are not his primary interests. Athanasius apparently knows what kind of "meaning" his friend is seeking in the Psalms. Marcellinus is not interested in honing his talents as an exegete or a polemicist, but in discovering what the Psalter is in relation to the rest of Scripture, and how and when the particular psalms are to be used in the life of Christians. Athanasius, accordingly, does not answer him as a biblical commentator. There are no lengthy discussions of etymologies, no attempts to work systematically through a psalm in order to analyze the author's intent—the technical and interpretive queries of the scientific exegete are not operative. Nor do we see marshaling of proof-texts, which Athanasius does so brilliantly in the anti-Arian treatises. Here Athanasius writes as pastor and the giver of spiritual and moral counsel. The letter's purpose is to instruct and advise. In its approach and tone it is most like the bishop's annual festal epistles, in which biblical quotations serve to warn, chasten, and encourage.[33]

The Letter's Design

A curious literary device frames Athanasius's answer to Marcellinus. As if to add authority and mystery to his words, Athanasius presents the discussion as the monologue of "a learned old man" (chap. 1). This "old master of the Psalter" reveals the plan of his remarks in likening the Book of Psalms to a garden: It contains the things found in other biblical books, but possesses its own beauties in addition—and these in song. In chapters 3–8 a demonstration is given of the Psalter's recapitulation of themes found in the Law and the Prophets—creation, liberation from Egypt, and so forth. The writings of the Prophets and their parallel prophetic psalms are treated in a way consistent with earlier and later Christian practice. They function as oracles—as predictions, confirmed by history, of Christ's birth, ministry, passion, ascension, and coming appearance as judge.[34]

A second section (chaps. 10–13) contains an intriguing argument for the uniqueness of the Book of Psalms. The old man claims that in a way that distinguishes the Psalter from the rest of Scripture, the Psalms are immediate, direct, and capable of being spoken as one's own words. Their phrases "become like a mirror to the person singing them, so that he might perceive himself and the emotions of his soul" (chap. 12). The assertion follows that in its capacity to accommodate to human disposition and to direct the soul, the Psalter is like Christ's incarnation and exemplary life.

The main portion of the letter (chaps. 14–26) is taken up with the classification of psalms. Here Athanasius addresses Marcellinus's desire to know each psalm's meaning. Psalms are prescribed for a range of human situations and crises. The prescriptions are based not only on the needs of persons in particular straits and circumstances, but also on God's actions and the responses they require. So attention is given to the use of particular psalms for the remembrance of "the kind acts of God accomplished for the fathers" of Israel (chap. 19) and "the benefits won for us by the Savior through his sufferings" (chap. 26). There is no attempt to lay bare the sense of any psalm line by line, nor is there any concern to understand the Psalms in their own historical context (for a patristic writer, the age of David). Athanasius is intent on suggesting the meaning Marcellinus was seeking—namely, the efficacy of each psalm, the distinctive power each offers to the Christian believer and worshiper.

A distinct shift occurs in the concluding chapters (27–33), where it is clear that known misunderstandings and abuses of the Psalter are being corrected. Athanasius's old man explains what is deficient in the view that music and singing in worship are "for the sake of the ear's delight" (chap. 27), and he warns against those who "amplify [the] words of the Psalter with the persuasive phrases of the profane" (chap. 31). How are the saints of old (and the Spirit who speaks in them) to join you in your prayer if their words and phrases are made unfamiliar to them?

Spirit and Spirituality in the Letter

From beginning to end, the *Letter to Marcellinus* takes for granted the power that resides in the Book of Psalms and the benefit that accrues to men and women who recite them. It cannot be said that the Psalter is more holy than the other holy writings, but Athanasius does insist that God honors the supplications made in the words of the Psalms, that the Spirit works through the Psalms both to stir up and to moderate the emotions, and to provide "the perfect image for the souls' course of life" (chap. 14).

Through the *Letter to Marcellinus* moderns gain a sense of the piety of fourth-century Christians in the Eastern Mediterranean—of the formal and formulaic as well as the personal and immediate elements in public and private prayer. The document testifies on every page to Athanasius's conviction, which he sought to foster in those to whom he was pastor, of the central and sustaining force of the recitation of the Psalms in the experience of Christian people.

Translating the Letter to Marcellinus

The Greek text of *Epistula ad Marcellinum de interpretatione Psalmorum* is found in Migne's *Patrologia Graeca* 27 (1887), columns 11–46.

A German translation exists: J. Fisch, *Des heiligen Athanasius Brief an Marcellinus über die Erklärung der Psalmen*, in *Des heiligen Athanasius ausgewählte Schriften* 2, Bibliothek der Kirchenväter (Kempten: Jos. Kösel'schen Buchhandlung, 1875), pp. 331–366.

25

INTRODUCTION

As in the translation of the *Vita Antonii*, biblical citations from the New Testament are given in the translation of the Revised Standard Version and those from the Old Testament are adapted from Brenton's translation of the Septuagint. Athanasius's letter reflects the Septuagint's numbering of the Psalms, which is followed here in the text and in the notes.

ATHANASIUS

THE LIFE OF ANTONY
AND
THE LETTER TO MARCELLINUS

THE CLASSICS OF WESTERN SPIRITUALITY

The Life and Affairs of our Holy Father Antony
(Written and dispatched to the monks abroad)[1]

INTRODUCTION

You have entered on a fine contest with the monks in Egypt, intending as you do to measure up to or even to surpass them in your discipline of virtue. For by now you have monasteries, and the name of the monks carries public weight.[2] One may justly praise this purpose of yours, and as you ask in prayer, may God bring your requests to fulfillment.

Since you have asked me about the career of the blessed Antony, hoping to learn how he began the discipline, who he was before this, and what sort of death he experienced, and if the things said concerning him are true—so that you also might lead yourselves in imitation of him—I received your directive with ready good will. For simply to remember Antony is a great profit and assistance for me also. I know that even in hearing, along with marveling at the man, you will want also to emulate his purpose, for Antony's way of life provides monks with a sufficient picture for ascetic practice. Do not be incredulous about what you hear of him from those who make reports. Consider, rather, that from them only a few of his feats have been learned, for these hardly gave full description of so much. And even if, persuaded by you, I sent as much as

I could convey through the letter, recalling a few of the things about him, do not fail to put questions to those who sail from here. For perhaps after each tells what he knows, the account concerning him would still scarcely do him justice.

It was my hope, when I received your letter, to send for some of the monks who were more accustomed to being near him, so that after learning something more, I might send you a fuller narrative. But since the season for sailing was coming to a close, and the letter-bearer was eager—for this reason, what I myself know (for I have seen him often) and what I was able to learn from him when I followed him more than a few times and poured water over his hands,[3] I hastened to write to your piety. In every instance I kept my mind fixed on the truth, lest someone disbelieve because he heard too much, or lest, on the contrary, learning less than he ought to, he regard the man with contempt.

THE LIFE OF ST. ANTONY

Pre-monastic life
251-71

1. Antony was an Egyptian by race. His parents were well born and prosperous, and since they were Christians, he also was reared in a Christian manner. When he was a child he lived with his parents, cognizant of little else besides them and his home. As he grew and became a boy, and was advancing in years, he could not bear to learn letters, wishing also to stand apart from friendship with other children. All his yearning, as it has been written of Jacob,[4] was for living, an unaffected person, in his home. Of course he accompanied his parents to the Lord's house, and as a child he was not frivolous, nor as a youth did he grow contemptuous; rather, he was obedient to his mother and father, and paying attention to the readings, he carefully

took to heart what was profitable in them. And although he lived as a child in relative affluence, he did not pester his parents for food of various and luxurious kinds, nor did he seek the pleasures associated with food, but with merely the things he found before him he was satisfied, and he looked for nothing more.

2. He was left alone, after his parents' death, with one quite young sister. He was about eighteen or even twenty years old, and he was responsible both for the home and his sister. Six months had not passed since the death of his parents when, going to the Lord's house as usual and gathering his thoughts, he considered while he walked how the apostles, forsaking everything, followed the Savior, and how in Acts some sold what they possessed and took the proceeds and placed them at the feet of the apostles for distribution among those in need, and what great hope is stored up for such people in heaven.[5] He went into the church pondering these things, and just then it happened that the Gospel was being read, and he heard the Lord saying to the rich man, *If you would be perfect, go, sell what you possess and give to the poor, and you will have treasure in heaven.*[6] It was as if by God's design he held the saints in his recollection, and as if the passage were read on his account. Immediately Antony went out from the Lord's house and gave to the townspeople the possessions he had from his forebears (three hundred fertile and very beautiful *arourae*[7]), so that they would not disturb him or his sister in the least. And selling all the rest that was portable, when he collected sufficient money, he donated it to the poor, keeping a few things for his sister.

3. But when, entering the Lord's house once more, he heard in the Gospel the Lord saying, *Do not be anxious about tomorrow,* he could not remain any longer, but going out he gave those remaining possessions also to the needy. Placing

his sister in the charge of respected and trusted virgins, and giving her over to the convent for rearing, he devoted himself from then on to the discipline rather than the household, giving heed to himself and patiently training himself. There were not yet many monasteries in Egypt, and no monk knew at all the great desert, but each of those wishing to give attention to his life disciplined himself in isolation, not far from his own village. Now at that time in the neighboring village there was an old man who had practiced from his youth the solitary life. When Antony saw him, he emulated him in goodness.[8] At first he also began by remaining in places proximate to his village. And going forth from there, if he heard of some zealous person anywhere, he searched him out like the wise bee. He did not go back to his own place unless he had seen him, and as though receiving from him certain supplies for traveling the road to virtue, he returned. Spending the beginning stages of his discipline in that place, then, he weighed in his thoughts how he would not look back on things of his parents, nor call his relatives to memory. All the desire and all the energy he possessed concerned the exertion of the discipline. He worked with his hands, though, having heard that he who is idle, *let him not eat.*[9] And he spent what he made partly for bread, and partly on those in need. He prayed constantly, since he learned that it is necessary to pray unceasingly in private.[10] For he paid such close attention to what was read that nothing from Scripture did he fail to take in—rather he grasped everything, and in him the memory took the place of books.

4. Leading his life in this way, Antony was loved by all. He was sincerely obedient to those men of zeal he visited, and he considered carefully the advantage in zeal and in ascetic living that each held in relation to him. He observed the graciousness of one, the eagerness for prayers in an-

other; he took careful note of one's freedom from anger, and the human concern of another. And he paid attention to one while he lived a watchful life, or one who pursued studies, as also he admired one for patience, and another for fastings and sleeping on the ground. The gentleness of one and the long-suffering of yet another he watched closely. He marked, likewise, the piety toward Christ and the mutual love of them all. And having been filled in this manner, he returned to his own place of discipline, from that time gathering the attributes of each in himself, and striving to manifest in himself what was best from all. Even toward those of his own age he was not contentious, with the sole exception of his desire that he appear to be second to none of them in moral improvements. And this he did so as to grieve no one, but even to have them rejoice for him. All those, then, who were from his village and those good people with whom he associated, seeing him living thus, used to call him "God-loved," and some hailed him as "son," and some as "brother."

5. The devil, who despises and envies good, could not bear seeing such purpose in a youth, but the sort of things he had busied himself in doing in the past, he set to work to do against this person as well. First he attempted to lead him away from the discipline, suggesting memories of his possessions, the guardianship of his sister, the bonds of kinship, love of money and of glory, the manifold pleasure of food, the relaxations of life, and, finally, the rigor of virtue, and how great the labor is that earns it, suggesting also the bodily weakness and the length of time involved. So he raised in his mind a great dust cloud of considerations, since he wished to cordon him off from his righteous intention. But the enemy saw his own weakness in the face of Antony's resolve, and saw that he instead was being thrown for a fall by the sturdiness of this contestant, and

being overturned by his great faith and falling over Antony's constant prayers. Then he placed his confidence in the weapons *in the navel of his belly*,[11] and boasting in these (for they constitute his first ambush against the young), he advanced against the youth, noisily disturbing him by night, and so troubling him in the daytime that even those who watched were aware of the bout that occupied them both. The one hurled foul thoughts and the other overturned them through his prayers; the former resorted to titillation, but the latter, seeming to blush, fortified the body with faith and with prayers and fasting. And the beleaguered devil undertook one night to assume the form of a woman and to imitate her every gesture, solely in order that he might beguile Antony. But in thinking about the Christ and considering the excellence won through him, and the intellectual part of the soul,[12] Antony extinguished the fire of his opponent's deception. Once again the enemy cast before him the softness of pleasure, but he, angered and saddened (as we might expect), pondered the threat of the fire of judgment and the worm's work, and setting these in opposition, he passed through these testings unharmed. All these were things that took place to the enemy's shame. For he who considered himself to be like God was now made a buffoon by a mere youth, and he who vaunted himself against flesh and blood was turned back by a flesh-bearing man. Working with Antony was the Lord, who bore flesh for us, and gave to the body the victory over the devil, so that each of those who truly struggle can say, It is *not I, but the grace of God which is in me.*[13]

6. Finally, then, when the dragon was unable by this strategy to defeat him, but instead saw himself being thrust from Antony's heart, he gnashed his teeth (as Scripture says), and as he altered himself, taking on the likeness of his mind, it was in the visage of a black boy that he afterwards

The devil appears to Antony as a woman and a black boy! among others. Why?

manifested himself.[14] And as if succumbing, he no longer attacked by means of thoughts (for the crafty one had been cast out), but using now a human voice, said, "I tricked many, and I vanquished many, but just now, waging my attack on you and your labors, as I have upon many others, I was too weak." Antony asked, "You who are saying these things to me, who are you?" And immediately he emitted pitiful shouts, and said, "I am the friend of fornication. I set its ambushes and I worked its seductions against the young—I have even been called the spirit of fornication. How many who wanted to live prudently I have deceived! How many of those exercising self-control I won over when I agitated them! I am the one on whose account the prophet reprimands those who fall, saying, you have *been led astray by a spirit of fornication.*[15] For it was by my devices that they were tripped. I am he who so frequently troubled you and so many times was overturned by you." And Antony gave thanks to the Lord, and responding boldly to him, said: "You, then, are much to be despised, for you are black of mind, and like a powerless child. From now on you cause me no anxiety, for *the Lord is my helper, and I shall look upon my enemies.*[16] Hearing these words, the black one immediately fled, cowering at the words and afraid even to approach the man.

7. This was Antony's first contest against the devil—or, rather, this was in Antony the success of the Savior, who *condemned sin in the flesh, in order that the just requirement of the Law might be fulfilled in us, who walk not according to the flesh but according to the Spirit.*[17] But Antony did not then become careless or arrogant, as though the devil were conquered, nor did the enemy, like someone who had failed, cease from setting traps. For once again he was prowling around like a lion seeking some opportunity for attack. From the Scriptures Antony learned that the treacheries of

the enemy are numerous, and he practiced the discipline with intensity, realizing that although his foe had not been powerful enough to beguile him with bodily pleasure, he would surely attempt to entrap him by some other method, for the demon is a lover of sin. More and more then he mortified the body and kept it under subjection,[18] so that he would not, after conquering some challenges, trip up in others. So he made plans to accustom himself to more stringent practices, and many marveled, but he bore the labor with ease. For the eagerness that resided so long in his soul produced a good disposition in him, so that when he received from others even a small suggestion, he showed great enthusiasm for it. His watchfulness was such that he often passed the entire night without sleep, and doing this not once, but often, he inspired wonder. He ate once daily, after sunset, but there were times when he received food every second and frequently even every fourth day. His food was bread and salt, and for drinking he took only water. There is no reason even to speak of meat and wine, when indeed such a thing was not found among the other zealous men. A rush mat was sufficient to him for sleeping, but more regularly he lay on the bare ground. He disapproved of oil for anointing the skin, saying that it was more fitting for youths to hold to the ascetic life intensely, and not to seek the things that relax the body, but to habituate it to labors, thinking of the Apostle's remark, *When I am weak, then I am strong.*[19] For he said the soul's intensity is strong when the pleasures of the body are weakened. And this tenet of his was also truly wonderful, that neither the way of virtue nor separation from the world for its sake ought to be measured in terms of time spent, but by the aspirant's desire and purposefulness. He, indeed, did not hold time passed in his memory, but day by day, as if making a beginning of his asceticism, increased his exertion for advance, saying continually to himself Paul's word about *forgetting what lies behind and straining forward to what lies ahead,*[20] and recalling also the passage in which Elijah the prophet says, *the Lord . . . lives, before whom I stand today.*[21] He observed that in saying *today* he was not counting the time passed, but as one always establishing a beginning, he endeavored each day to present himself as the sort of person ready to appear before God—that is, pure of heart and prepared to obey his will, and no other. And he used to tell himself that from the career of the great Elijah, as from a mirror, the ascetic must always acquire knowledge of his own life.

8. Girding himself in this way, Antony went out to the ⟨ *Tombs* tombs that were situated some distance from the village. He charged one of his friends to supply him periodically with bread, and he entered one of the tombs and remained alone within, his friend having closed the door on him. When the enemy could stand it no longer—for he was apprehensive that Antony might before long fill the desert with the discipline—approaching one night with a multitude of demons he whipped him with such force that he lay on the earth, speechless from the tortures. He contended that the pains were so severe as to lead one to say that the blows could not have been delivered by humans, since they caused such agony. But by God's providence (for the Lord does not overlook those who place their hope in him), the friend came the next day bringing him the loaves. Opening the door and seeing him lying, as if dead, on the ground, he picked him up and carried him to the Lord's house in the village, and laid him on the earth. And many of his relatives and the people of the village stationed themselves by Antony as beside a corpse. But around midnight, coming to his senses and wakening, Antony, as he saw everyone sleeping, and only his friend keeping the watch, beckoned

to him and asked him to lift him again and carry him to the tombs, waking no one.

9. So he was taken back there by the man and, as before, the door was closed. Again he was alone inside. Because of the blows he was not strong enough to stand, but he prayed while lying down. And after the prayer he yelled out: "Here I am—Antony! I do not run from your blows, for even if you give me more, nothing shall separate me from the love of Christ."[22] Then he also sang, *Though an army should set itself in array against me, my heart shall not be afraid.*[23] These things, then, the ascetic thought and spoke, but the enemy who despises good, astonished that even after the blows he had received he dared to return, summoned his dogs and said, exploding with rage, "You see that we failed to stop this man with a spirit of fornication or with lashes. Far from it—he is even insolent to us. Let us approach him in another way." Now schemes for working evil come easily to the devil, so when it was nighttime they made such a crashing noise that that whole place seemed to be shaken by a quake. The demons, as if breaking through the building's four walls, and seeming to enter through them, were changed into the forms of beasts and reptiles. The place immediately was filled with the appearances of lions, bears, leopards, bulls, and serpents, asps, scorpions and wolves, and each of these moved in accordance with its form. The lion roared, wanting to spring at him; the bull seemed intent on goring; the creeping snake did not quite reach him; the onrushing wolf made straight for him—and altogether the sounds of all the creatures that appeared were terrible, and their ragings were fierce. Struck and wounded by them, Antony's body was subject to yet more pain. But unmoved and even more watchful in his soul he lay there, and he groaned because of the pain felt in his body, but being in control of his thoughts and as

if mocking them, he said: "If there were some power among you, it would have been enough for only one of you to come. But since the Lord has broken your strength, you attempt to terrify me by any means with the mob; it is a mark of your weakness that you mimic the shapes of irrational beasts." And again with boldness he said, "If you are able, and you did receive authority over me, don't hold back, but attack. But if you are unable, why, when it is vain, do you disturb me? For faith in our Lord is for us a seal and a wall of protection." So after trying many strategies, they gnashed their teeth because of him, for they made fools not of him, but of themselves.

10. In this circumstance also the Lord did not forget the wrestling of Antony, but came to his aid. For when he looked up he saw the roof being opened, as it seemed, and a certain beam of light descending toward him.[24] Suddenly the demons vanished from view, the pain of his body ceased instantly, and the building was once more intact. Aware of the assistance and both breathing more easily and relieved from the sufferings, Antony entreated the vision that appeared, saying, "Where were you? Why didn't you appear in the beginning, so that you could stop my distresses?" And a voice came to him: "I was here, Antony, but I waited to watch your struggle. And now, since you persevered and were not defeated, I will be your helper forever, and I will make you famous everywhere." On hearing this, he stood up and prayed, and he was so strengthened that he felt that his body contained more might than before. And he was about thirty-five years old at that time.

11. Going out the next day from the tomb, he was even more enthusiastic in his devotion to God, and meeting the old man mentioned earlier, he asked him to live with him in the wilderness. But when he declined, both be-

Outer Mountain

286–313

39

cause of his advanced age and because such a practice was not yet customary, Antony set out immediately for the mountain. Once more the enemy, observing his zeal and hoping to thwart it, threw in his path the apparition of a great silver dish. But Antony, knowing the craft of the despiser of goodness, stood looking at the dish and exposed the devil in it, saying, "A dish here in the wilderness? Where did it come from? This way has not been traveled, nor is there a trace of any travelers here. Since it is large, it could not have been missed if it fell. Or if it had been, the person who lost it would have found it when he returned and searched, since this place is desert. This is the craft of the devil. You will not frustrate my purpose by this, Devil! Take this with you to destruction!" As soon as he said this, it vanished like smoke from a fire.

12. And as he continued, he saw next no illusion, but actual gold thrown in his path. It is not clear whether the enemy pointed it out, or whether some more excellent power was training the athlete and demonstrating to the devil that he was not, in fact, concerned about money. This he did not relate, nor do we know the answer—only that what appeared was gold. So Antony marveled at the amount, but as one stepping over fire he passed it without turning. Indeed he hurried at such a pace that soon the place was hidden to view and unseen. Intensifying more and more his purpose, he hurried toward the mountain. When he discovered beyond the river a deserted fortress, empty so long that reptiles filled it, he went there, and took up residence in it. Then at once the creeping things departed, as if someone were in pursuit, and barricading the entrance once more, and putting aside enough loaves for six months (for the Thebans do this, and frequently they remain unspoiled for a whole year), and having water inside,

he was hidden within as in a shrine. He remained alone in the place, neither going out himself nor seeing any of those who visited. For a long time he continued this life of discipline, receiving the loaves twice yearly from the housetop above.

13. Since he did not allow them to enter, those of his acquaintance who came to him often spent days and nights outside. They heard what sounded like clamoring mobs inside making noises, emitting pitiful sounds and crying out, "Get away from what is ours! What do you have to do with the desert? You cannot endure our treachery!" At first those who were outside thought certain men were doing battle with him, and that these had gained entry by ladders, but when they stooped to peek through a hole, they saw no one, and they realized then that the adversaries were demons. They were frightened and they called Antony, and he heard them, but he disregarded the demons. And coming close to the door, he urged the men to be on their way and not to fear. "In this manner," he said, "the demons create apparitions and set them loose on those who are cowardly. For it is against the cowardly," he said, "that the demons create apparitions in this way. Therefore, seal yourselves with the sign and depart with confidence. And leave them to mock themselves." So they went away, fortified by the sign of the cross. Antony remained and suffered no injury from the demons, and neither did he grow tired of the contest. The support that was his through visions from above, along with the adversaries' weakness, brought much relief from his travails, and prepared him for greater zeal. His friends used to visit regularly, thinking they might find him dead, and they heard him singing, *Let God arise, and let his enemies be scattered; and let them that hate him flee from before him. As smoke vanishes, let them vanish; as wax*

melts before the fire, so let the sinners perish from before God.[25] And this as well: *All nations compassed me about; but in the name of the Lord I repulsed them.*[26]

14. Nearly twenty years he spent in this manner pursuing the ascetic life by himself, not venturing out and only occasionally being seen by anyone. After this, when many possessed the desire and will to emulate his asceticism, and some of his friends came and tore down and forcefully removed the fortress door, Antony came forth as though from some shrine, having been led into divine mysteries and inspired by God. This was the first time he appeared from the fortress for those who came out to him. And when they beheld him, they were amazed to see that his body had maintained its former condition, neither fat from lack of exercise, nor emaciated from fasting and combat with demons, but was just as they had known him prior to his withdrawal. The state of his soul was one of purity, for it was not constricted by grief, nor relaxed by pleasure, nor affected by either laughter or dejection. Moreover, when he saw the crowd, he was not annoyed any more than he was elated at being embraced by so many people. He maintained utter equilibrium, like one guided by reason and steadfast in that which accords with nature. Through him the Lord healed many of those present who suffered from bodily ailments; others he purged of demons, and to Antony he gave grace in speech. Thus he consoled many who mourned, and others hostile to each other he reconciled in friendship,[27] urging everyone to prefer nothing in the world above the love of Christ. And when he spoke and urged them to keep in mind the future goods and the affection in which we are held by God, *who did not spare his own Son, but gave him up for us all,*[28] he persuaded many to take up the solitary life. And so, from then on, there were monasteries in the mountains and the desert

was made a city by monks, who left their own people and registered themselves for the citizenship in the heavens.

15. Once he had to cross the canal of Arsinoë (his visitation of the brothers was the cause), and the canal was full of crocodiles.[29] And after simply praying, he and those in his company entered it and passed through unharmed. Returning to his cell, he carried on the same holy and active labors. Through regular conversation he strengthened the resolve of those who were already monks, and stirred most of the others to a desire for the discipline, and before long, by the attraction of his speech, a great many monasteries came into being, and like a father he guided them all.

16. One day when he had gone out, all the monks came to him, asking to hear a discourse. In the Egyptian tongue he told them these things. "The Scriptures are sufficient for instruction, but it is good for us to encourage each other in the faith. Now you, saying what you know, bring this to the father like children, and I, as your elder, will share what I know and the fruits of my experience. In the first place, let us hold in common the same eagerness not to surrender what we have begun, either by growing fainthearted in the labors or by saying, 'We have spent a long time in the discipline.' Rather, as though making a beginning daily, let us increase our dedication. For the entire life span of men is very brief when measured against the ages to come, so that all our time is nothing in comparison with eternal life. Everything in the world is sold for what it is worth, and someone trades an item for its equivalent. But the promise of eternal life is purchased for very little. For it is written: *The days of our lives have seventy years in them, but if men should be in strength, eighty years, and what is more than these would be labor and trouble.*[30] When, therefore, we live the whole eighty years, or even a hundred in the discipline, these hundred are not equal to the years we

43

shall reign, for instead of a hundred we shall reign forever
and ever. And even though we have been contestants on
earth, we do not receive our inheritance on earth, but we
possess the promises in heaven. Putting off the body, then,
which is corruptible, we receive it back incorruptible.[31]

17. "Therefore, my children, let us not lose heart. Let
us not think that the time is too long or what we do is
great, *for the sufferings of this present time are not worth comparing with the glory that is to be revealed to us.*[32] And let us
not consider, when we look at the world, that we have given up things of some greatness, for even the entire earth is
itself quite small in relation to all of heaven. If now it happened that we were lords of all the earth, and renounced all
the earth, that would amount to nothing as compared with
the kingdom of heaven. For just as if someone might despise one copper drachma in order to gain a hundred gold
drachmas, so he who is ruler of the whole earth, and renounces it, loses little, and he receives a hundred times
more. But if all the earth is not equal in value to the heavens, then he who has given up a few *arourae* sacrifices virtually nothing, and even if he should give up a house or
considerable wealth, he has no reason to boast or grow
careless. We ought also to realize that if we do not surrender these things through virtue, then later when we die we
shall leave these things behind—often, to those whom we
do not wish, as Ecclesiastes reminds us.[33] This being the
case, why should we not give them up for virtue's sake, so
that we might inherit even a kingdom? Let none among us
have even the yearning to possess. For what benefit is there
in possessing these things that we do not take with us?
Why not rather own those things that we are able to take
away with us—such things as prudence, justice, temperance, courage, understanding, love, concern for the poor,
faith in Christ, freedom from anger, hospitality? If we pos-

renunciation

sess these, we shall discover them running before, preparing hospitality for us there in the land of the meek.

18. "With these thoughts let a person convince himself not to grow careless, especially if he considers himself to be the Lord's servant, obliged to do his master's will. Just as a servant would not dare to say, 'Since I worked yesterday, I am not working today,' nor, counting the time that has passed, relax in the days ahead; but each day, as it is written in the Gospel,[34] he shows the same eagerness in order to please his lord and avoid peril—so also let us persist daily in the ascetic life, knowing that if we are lax even one day, the Lord will not forgive us on the basis of past performance, but will direct his wrath against us because of our neglect. So have we heard in Ezekiel;[35] and so also we see in the case of Judas, who destroyed in one night what he had achieved in the preceding time.

19. "Therefore, my children, let us hold to the discipline, and not be careless. For we have the Lord for our co-worker in this, as it is written, God *works for good with* everyone who chooses the good.[36] And in order that we not become negligent, it is good to carefully consider the Apostle's statement: *I die daily.*[37] For if we so live as people dying daily, we will not commit sin. The point of the saying is this: As we rise daily, let us suppose that we shall not survive till evening, and again, as we prepare for sleep, let us consider that we shall not awaken. By its very nature our life is uncertain, and is meted out daily by providence. If we think this way, and in this way live—daily—we will not sin, nor will we crave anything, nor bear a grudge against anyone, nor will we lay up treasures on earth, but as people who anticipate dying each day we shall be free of possessions, and we shall forgive all things to all people. The desire for a woman, or another sordid pleasure, we shall not merely control—rather, we shall turn from it as

something transitory, forever doing battle and looking toward the day of judgment. For the larger fear and dread of the torments always destroys pleasure's smooth allure, and rouses the declining soul.

20. "Having therefore made a beginning, and set out already on the way of virtue, let us press forward to what lies ahead.[38] And let none turn back as Lot's wife did, especially since the Lord said, *No one who puts his hand to the plow and* turns *back is fit for the Kingdom of heaven.*[39] Now 'turning back' is nothing except feeling regret and once more thinking about things of the world. But do not be afraid to hear about virtue, and do not be a stranger to the term. For it is not distant from us, nor does it stand external to us, but its realization lies in us, and the task is easy if only we shall will it. Now the Greeks leave home and traverse the sea in order to gain an education, but there is no need for us to go abroad on account of the Kingdom of heaven, nor to cross the sea for virtue. For the Lord has told us before, *the Kingdom of God is within you.*[40] All virtue needs, then, is our willing, since it is in us, and arises from us. For virtue exists when the soul maintains its intellectual part according to nature. It holds fast according to nature when it remains as it was made—and it was made beautiful and perfectly straight. It was for this reason that Joshua, son of Nun, when exhorting the people, said: *Set your heart straight toward the Lord God of Israel.*[41] John's urging was: *Make your paths straight.*[42] As far as the soul is concerned, being straight consists in its intellectual part's being according to nature, as it was created. But when it turns from its course and is twisted away from what it naturally is, then we speak of the vice of the soul. So the task is not difficult, for if we remain as we were made, we are in virtue, but if we turn our thoughts toward contemptible things, we are condemned as evil. If the task depended on

something external that must be procured, it would be truly difficult, but since the matter centers in us, let us protect ourselves from sordid ideas, and, since we have received it as a trust, let us preserve the soul for the Lord, so that he may recognize his work as being just the same as he made it.

21. "Let the contest be ours, so that anger does not rule us or desire overwhelm us, for it is written: *The anger of man does not work the righteousness of God*, and *desire, when it has conceived, gives birth to sin; and sin, when it is full grown, brings forth death*.[43] Conducting our lives in this manner, let us carefully keep watch, and as Scripture says, let us *keep our heart in all watchfulness*.[44] For we have terrible and villainous enemies—the evil demons, and our *contending* is against these, as the Apostle said—*not against flesh and blood, but against the principalities, against the powers, against the world rulers of this present darkness, against the spiritual hosts of wickedness in the heavenly places*.[45] So the mob of them is great in the air around us, and they are not far from us. But the difference between them is great. A speech about their natures and distinctions would be lengthy, and such a discourse is for others greater than us. For the present, that which is pressing and necessary for us is simply to know their unscrupulous tricks against us.

22. "First we ought to understand this: The demons were not created as the figures we now identify by 'demon,' for God made nothing bad. They were made good, but falling from the heavenly wisdom and thereafter wandering around the earth, they deceived the Greeks through apparitions. And envious of us Christians, they meddle with all things in their desire to frustrate our journey into heaven, so that we might not ascend to the place from which they themselves fell. Therefore much prayer and asceticism is needed so that one who receives through the

47

Spirit the gift of discrimination of spirits might be able to recognize their traits[46]—for example, which of them are less wicked, and which more; and in what kind of pursuit each of them exerts himself, and how each of them is overturned and expelled. For numerous are their treacheries and the moves in their plot. The blessed apostle and his companions recognized these when they said, *We are not ignorant of his designs*,[47] and on the basis of our testings by them, we ought to set each other on the right path, away from them. Therefore I, having had my share of trial from them, address you as my children.

23. "Should they see any Christians—monks, especially—laboring gladly and advancing, they first attack and tempt them, placing stumbling blocks in the way. Their stumbling blocks consist of evil thoughts. But we need not fear their suggestions, for by prayers and fasting and by faith in the Lord they are brought down immediately. But even after they fall they do not cease, but approach again, with malice and cunning. When they are unable to deceive the heart by conspicuous and filthy pleasure, again they make another kind of assault, and pretend to frighten it by fabricating phantasms, transforming themselves, and imitating women, beasts, reptiles, and huge bodies and thousands of soldiers. Nevertheless we need not fear their apparitions, for they are nothing and they disappear quickly—especially if one fortifies himself with faith and the sign of the cross. To be sure, they are daring and completely shameless, for if they are thus conquered, they simply attack again in another way. They pretend to prophesy and to predict things to come, and they appear to be as tall as a roof and vast in width, so that those they were unable to lead astray with thoughts they might deviously snatch away by means of the phantasms. But should they in this

case also find the soul secure in the faith and the hopeful purpose, then they bring forward their leader."

24. Antony continued: "Frequently they appear to be like the devil, which the Lord revealed to Job saying, *His eyes are like the appearance of the morning star. Out of his mouth proceed burning lamps and hearths of fire are cast forth. Out of his nostrils proceeds smoke of a furnace burning with fire of coals. His breath is live coals, and a flame goes out of his mouth.*[48] When the prince of the demons appears in this form, the deceitful one seeks to terrify, as I said earlier, making grand statements, as the Lord described him to Job saying, *For he considers iron as chaff, and brass as rotten wood . . . and he regards the sea as a pot of ointment, and the lowest part of the deep as a captive; he reckons the deep as a place for walking,*[49] and through the prophet, *The enemy said: I will pursue, I will overtake,*[50] and through another, *and I will take with my hand all the world as a nest, and I will even take them as eggs that have been left.*[51] In short, they set about their boasting with claims of this sort, and they profess them in order to deceive the pious. But again there is no need for us, the faithful, to fear his manifestations nor to worry about his words, for he lies—he speaks no truth whatever. Although he speaks such and so many things, and is overbold, never mind—like a serpent he was drawn in with a hook by the Savior, and like a beast of burden he received a halter around the snout, and like a runaway he was bound by a ring for his nostrils, and his lips were pierced by an iron clasp.[52] He was also bound by the Lord like a sparrow, to receive our mockery.[53] And, like scorpions and snakes, he and his fellow demons have been put in a position to be trampled underfoot by us Christians. The evidence of this is that we now conduct our lives in opposition to him. For he who threatened to dry up the sea and seize the world,

take note that now he is unable to hinder your asceticism, or even my speaking against him. Therefore let us not pay attention to what he might say—for he lies—nor let us be frightened by his apparitions, which themselves are also deceptions. What appears in them is not true light; rather, they contain the initial elements and likenesses of the fire prepared for them, and in those elements in which they are soon to be consumed they attempt to terrify mankind. They do, without doubt, appear, but they disappear again at once, harming none of the faithful, but carrying with themselves the likeness of the fire that is about to receive them. So here it is not necessary to fear them, for by the grace of Christ all their pursuits come to nothing.

25. "But they are treacherous and prepared to be changed and transformed into all shapes. Frequently, without becoming visible, they pretend to chant with sacred songs, and they recite sayings from the Scriptures. And even when we are reading, they are able to say right away and repeatedly, as if in echo, the same things we have read. While we are sleeping they arouse us for prayers, and they do this incessantly, hardly allowing us to sleep. It is possible, when they model themselves after the form of monks, for them to pretend to speak like the devout, so that by means of the similarity of form they deceive, and then drag those whom they have beguiled wherever they wish. Nevertheless it is unnecessary to heed them, even if they awaken you for prayer, or counsel you to eat nothing at all, or pretend to level accusations and reproaches concerning actions for which, at another time, they excused us. They do not do these things for the sake of piety or truth, but so that they might bring the simple to despair, and declare the discipline useless, and make men sick of the solitary life as something burdensome and very oppressive, and trip up those who, opposing them, lead it.

26. "The prophet sent by the Lord called such creatures wretched when he said, *Woe to him that gives his neighbor a troubled drink.*[54] For such practices and thoughts are
subversive of the way that leads to virtue. The Lord himself, even if the demons spoke the truth (for they said truly,
You are the Son of God),[55] still silenced them and prevented
their speaking, so they would not sow their own evil with
the truth, and in order that he might train us never to heed
such as these, even if they seem to speak the truth. For it is
not fitting for us, who possess the holy Scriptures and the
freedom of the Savior, to be taught by the devil, the one
who did not maintain his own rank,[56] but has turned his
mind in one direction after another. For this reason, even
when he utters sayings from the Scriptures, the Lord stops
him by saying: *But to the sinner God has said, Why do you declare my ordinances, and take up my covenant in your mouth?*[57]
For everything they do—they talk, they cause mass confusion, they pretend to be others than themselves, and they
create disturbances—all this is for the deception of the simple. They also make crashing sounds and laugh madly, and
hiss. But if one should pay no attention to them, they cry
out and lament as though vanquished.

27. "Therefore the Lord, as God, silenced the demons.
But it is fitting for us, since we have learned from the holy
ones, to act as they acted and to emulate their courage. For
when they saw these things, they used to say, *When the sinner stood in my presence, I was dumb, and humbled myself, and
kept silence from good words,*[58] and again, *But I, as a deaf man,
heard not; and was as a deaf man not opening his mouth. And I
was as a man that hears not.*[59] Therefore let us also pay them
no heed, treating them as strangers to us, and let us not
obey them, even in the event that they arouse us for prayer, or talk to us about fasting. Rather, let us devote ourselves to our own purpose in the discipline, and not be led

astray by them, though they do all things with cunning. We must not fear them, even though they seem to assault us or threaten us with death, for they are weak and have power to do nothing except hurl threats.

28. "I have so far spoken of this matter in passing, but now I must not hesitate to give a fuller account of the things concerning them, for the reminder will work for your safety.

"Since the Lord made his sojourn with us, the enemy is fallen and his powers have diminished. For this reason, though he is able to do nothing, nevertheless like a tyrant fallen from power he does not remain quiet, but issues threats, even if they are only words. Let every one of you consider this, and he will be empowered to treat the demons with contempt. Now if they were bound to bodies of the sort we have, they might have to say, 'We cannot find the men who hide themselves, but when we do find them, we inflict injury.' By hiding, then, we would be able to escape them, locking doors against them. However, even if they are not like this, but have the power to enter through locked doors, and they are met everywhere in the air—both they and their leader, the devil—and though they intend malice and are ready to do harm, and as the Savior said, 'The devil, the father of evil, is *a murderer from the begining*,'[60] nevertheless we are now living, and indeed we lead our lives in opposition to him. It is evident that they possess no strength! For a place does not prevent them from planning treachery, and they do not look on us as friends, in order to show us mercy, and they are not lovers of the good, with the intention of being reformed. On the contrary, they are evil, and they desire nothing so much as inflicting injury on those who love virtue and honor God. But because they have no power to act, they do nothing except issue threats. If they had the power, they would not delay, but immediately would perform the evil for which they have a ready inclination—especially evil directed against us. Take note, then, that we who are gathered here now speak against them, and they know that as we advance they are weakened. Indeed, if they had authority, they would not permit one of us Christians to live, for *godliness is an abomination to the sinner*.[61] But since they are powerless, they wound themselves instead, because the things they threaten they are unable to perform.

"To end our fear of them, we ought to ponder this: If the capability were theirs, they would not come in great mobs, nor create phantasms, nor would they work their fraud by being transfigured. It would suffice for only one to come and do what he can and wills—especially because everyone who actually possesses the power does not destroy with apparitions, nor arouse fear with large mobs, but exercises his might directly, as he wishes. The demons, however, unable to effect anything, play parts as if they were on stage, changing their forms and striking fear in children by the illusion of the hordes and their shapes. For these antics they deserve instead to be ridiculed as weaklings. The true angel of the Lord, at least, who was sent by the Lord to the Assyrians, had no need of hordes, nor of visible apparitions, nor of crashing sounds and rattling noises. He wielded his authority quietly, and at once destroyed a hundred and eighty-five thousand foes.[62] But the demons, who lack the power to do anything, these are the sort who must try to frighten, even if through illusions.

29. "Now if anyone considers the events of Job's life, and says: 'Why then did the devil set forth and do all those things to him? Did he not strip him of his possessions, destroy his children and *strike* him *with painful boils?*'[63]—let such a questioner know that the devil was not the one possessing strength, but it was God who turned over the test-

ing of Job to him. It is clear that because he was capable of doing nothing, he asked this, and when he was granted his request, he acted. So on this ground also the enemy is to be condemned, that even when he desired it, he did not prevail against one righteous man. If he possessed strength, he would not have made the request. But in asking—not once, but twice—he showed himself weak and capable of nothing. It is not remarkable if he had no might against Job, when indeed destruction would not befall even the man's cattle unless God allowed it. In fact, the devil has no authority over swine, for, as it is written in the Gospel, *they begged* the Lord, *saying,* 'Send *us to the swine.*'[64] But if they held no sway over the swine, how much less do they hold over people made in the image of God!

30. "We need, therefore, to fear God alone, holding them in contempt and fearing them not at all. Indeed, the more they do these things, let us all the more exert ourselves in the discipline that opposes them, for a great weapon against them is a just life and trust in God. They are afraid of the ascetics on several counts—for their fasting, the vigils, the prayers, the meekness and gentleness, the contempt for money, the lack of vanity, the humility, the love of the poor, the almsgiving, the freedom from wrath, and most of all for their devotion to Christ. It is for this reason that they do all they do—in order not to have those monks trampling them underfoot. For they know the grace that has been given to the faithful for combat against them by the Savior, in his saying, *Behold, I have given you authority to tread upon serpents and scorpions, and over all the power of the enemy.*[65]

31. "Furthermore, should they pretend to prophesy, let no one be won over. It frequently happens that they tell us days in advance about brothers who are to travel our way some days later—and these people do arrive. The de-

mons do this not out of any concern for their hearers, but in order to persuade them to trust them, and after that, having brought them under control, to destroy them. Therefore we must not pay attention to them, but overthrow them even while they are speaking, since we have no need of them. For what is so marvelous, if they who use bodies thinner in substance than those of humans, spying those who begin their journey, get a head start in the running and announce their arrival? This sort of thing someone riding a horse also foretells, preceding those who journey on foot. So it is not necessary to marvel at them in this case. They have no foreknowledge of things that have not yet occurred; God is the only one who knows *all things before their birth*.[66] But these, like thieves, run ahead and report what they see. To how many do they right now give signs regarding our affairs—that we are gathered together and that we are speaking against them—before someone could leave from among us and make a report! But some boy swift of foot could do this, outrunning one who is slower.

"What I am saying is this. Should someone begin to travel from the Thebaid, or from some other place, they do not know before he begins to walk if he will walk. But after they see him walking, they run ahead, and before he comes they announce him. And so it is that these travelers arrive after a few days. But often, when people on a journey turn back, the demons are caught in a lie.

32. "So, too, there are times when they talk nonsense about the water of the River. For when they observe numerous rains occurring in parts of Ethiopia, knowing how the flooding of the River originates there, before the water enters Egypt they rush ahead and report it. But even men could have told this, if they were able to run as fast as these. David's watchman, when he ascended to a height,

saw the person approaching better than the man who remained below,[67] and he, as the one running ahead, told before the others not the things that had not taken place but the things already underway and happening. In just that way these demons also choose to hurry ahead and declare signs to others for the sole purpose of deceiving. But if, meanwhile, providence plans something different concerning the waters or the travelers—for this is within its power—then the demons have spoken falsely, and those who have listened to them are deceived.

33. "So it was that the oracles of the Greeks arose and they were led astray in former times by the demons. But so also has this deceit been brought to an end from this time forward, for the Lord came, who reduced to impotency not only their villainy, but the demons themselves. For they know nothing by their own power, but like thieves they pass along what they pick up from others, and they are more nearly speculators than prognosticators. If, therefore, they sometimes speak the truth, do not let anyone marvel at them for this. It happens also that physicians who deal with illnesses, observing the same disease in different people, offer a prognosis, frequently conjecturing from what is familiar to them. And again, ships' helmsmen and farmers, looking at the weather conditions with practiced eyes, can predict if it will be stormy or fair. Now someone would not say on this account that they are foretelling through divine inspiration, but rather, on the basis of experience and practice. So if the demons also sometimes say these same things by conjecture, let no one, for this reason, be amazed at them or pay attention to them. For what good is it to the hearers to learn from them days in advance what is going to happen? And what is the purpose of the enthusiasm for knowing such things, even if one could, in truth, know them? This does not produce virtue, nor represent any evi-

dence at all of good character.[68] None of us is judged for what he does not know, any more than one is counted blessed because he is learned and possesses knowledge. It is rather in regard to these questions that each faces judgment: whether he has kept the faith and sincerely observed the commandments.

34. "Therefore we are not to attach much importance to these other things, and not for the purpose of gaining foreknowledge are we to train ourselves and labor—but rather in order that we may please God in the way we lead our lives. And we ought neither to pray that we might have the power to know things before they occur, nor ought we to ask this as a reward for our discipline—but rather that the Lord may be our fellow worker for the conquest of the devil. But if sometime the capacity for foreknowledge matters to us, let us be pure in understanding. For I believe that when a soul is pure in every way and in its natural state, it is able, having become clearsighted, to see more and farther than the demons, since it has the Lord who reveals things to it. Elisha's soul was like this, when it saw the things involving Giezi[69] and the armies that stood nearby.[70]

35."So when they come to you at night and they wish to tell what the future holds, or they say, 'We are the angels,' disregard them, for they are lying. And should they commend your asceticism and call you blessed, ignore them and have nothing at all to do with them. Instead, sign yourselves and your dwelling. And pray, and you will watch even as they become invisible. The truth is, they are cowards, and they are utterly terrified by the sign of the Lord's cross, because in it the Savior, stripping their armor, made an example of them.[71] But if they recklessly hold their ground, dancing around and producing various apparitions, neither dread them, nor cower in fear, nor pay attention to them on the chance that they are good.[72] For discrimination between the presence of the good and the evil is easy and possible, when God so grants it. A vision of the holy ones is not subject to disturbance, for *he will not wrangle or cry aloud, nor will any one hear his voice.*[73] But it comes with such tranquillity and gentleness that immediately joy and delight and courage enter the soul, for the Lord who is our joy, the power of God the Father,[74] accompanies them. And the thoughts of the soul remain untroubled and calm so that, shining brightly, it sees those who appear by its own light. The soul is overcome by a desire for divine and future realities, and it desires to be entirely united with these beings, if only it could depart in their company. But if some, being human, are frightened by the vision of the good spirits, those who appear remove their fear by means of love, as Gabriel did for Zacharias,[75] and the angel who appeared in the holy sepulchre did for the women,[76] and as did the one who said to the shepherds in the Gospel, *fear not.*[77] The fear of those people does not stem from the soul's cowardice, but from awareness of the presence of superior beings. Such, then, is the vision of the holy ones.

36. "The assault and appearance of the evil ones, on the other hand, is something troubling, with crashing and noise and shouting—the sort of disturbance one might expect from tough youths and robbers. From this come immediately terror of soul, confusion and disorder of thoughts, dejection, enmity toward ascetics, listlessness, grief, memory of relatives, and fear of death;[78] and finally there is craving for evil, contempt for virtue, and instability of character. When, therefore, you are frightened on seeing someone, if the fear is instantly removed, and its place is taken by unspeakable joy and cheerfulness and confidence and renewed strength, and calmness of

thought, and by the other things I mentioned before, both bravery and love of God, be of good courage and say your prayers. For the joy and the stability of the soul attest to the holiness of the one who is in your presence. So when Abraham saw the Lord he rejoiced, and John jumped for joy at the voice of Mary the God-bearer. But if, when certain ones appear, a disturbance occurs and noise from outside, and an apparition of a worldly kind, and threat of death, and things I spoke of before, know that the visit is from the wicked.

37. "And let this too be a sign to you: When the soul remains in fear, that is due to the presence of the enemies. For the demons do not remove the fear caused by such appearances, as the great Archangel Gabriel did for Mary and for Zacharias, and the angel who appeared at the tomb did for the women. On the contrary, when they see people who are fearful, they multiply the apparitions so as to terrify them all the more, and then descend in order to malign them, saying, 'Fall down and worship me.'[79] In this way they deceived the Greeks, who considered them to be gods, as they are falsely named. But the Lord did not allow us to be beguiled by the devil, and censuring him whenever he made such appearances, he said, *Begone, Satan! for it is written, 'You shall worship the Lord your God and him only shall you serve.'*[80] Therefore let the crafty one be despised by us more and more, for what the Lord has said, this he has done for our sakes, so that when the demons hear sayings of this sort from us they may be chased away through the Lord, who in these words censured them.

38. "We ought not to boast about expelling demons, nor become proud on account of healings performed; we are not to marvel only at him who casts out a demon, and treat with disdain him who does not. Let one learn well the discipline of each, and let him either copy and emulate it,

or correct it. For the performance of signs does not belong to us—this is the Savior's work. So he said to the disciples: *Do not rejoice that the* demons *are subject to you; but rejoice that your names are written in heaven.*[81] The fact that the names are written in heaven is a witness to our virtue and manner of life, but the ability to expel demons is itself a gift from the Savior, who bestowed it. So to those boasting, not in virtue, but in signs, and saying, *Lord, did we not cast out demons in your name, and do many mighty works in your name?*[82] he answered, 'Amen. I say to you, I do not know you!'[83] For the Lord does not know the ways of the ungodly.[84] Certainly one must pray, as I said earlier, to receive the gift of the discernment of spirits, so that we might not, as Scripture says, *believe every spirit.*[85]

39. "It was my wish to remain silent and to say nothing of my own contest, but be satisfied with these remarks alone. However, lest you think that I am talking about these things in general terms, and in order that you might be sure that I describe these matters from experience and fact—for this reason, even if I become like a fool (the Lord who hears me knows that my conscience is pure, and that it's not for myself, but for the sake of your love and advancement that I speak), I am telling you what cunning pursuits of the demons I myself have seen.[86] How many times they have called me blessed, and I cursed them in the Lord's name! How often they have prophesied about the water of the River, and I said to them: What concern is that of yours? Once they came with their threats and encircled me like warriors in battle array. On another occasion they filled my dwelling with horses and beasts and serpents, and I sang, *Some glory in chariots, and some in horses; but we will glory in the name of the Lord our God,*[87] and in these prayers they were repelled by the Lord. Once they came in darkness, having the appearance of light, and saying, 'We

have come to bring light to you, Antony.' But shutting my eyes, I prayed and immediately the light of the impious ones was extinguished. And after a few months they came as ones chanting and quoting from the Scriptures. *But I, as a deaf man, did not hear.*[88] Once they shook the cell, but I prayed, remaining unshaken in my purpose. And after these things, when they visited again, they made crashing noises, they whistled and they leaped about. As I prayed and lay chanting psalms to myself, they immediately began to wail and cry out, as though they were severely weakened, and I glorified the Lord, who came and made an example of their audacity and madness.

40. "Once a very tall demon appeared in an apparition and had the daring to say, 'I am the Power of God,' and 'I am Providence; what do you wish that I would give you?' But then, especially, I puffed at him, and speaking the name of Christ I made an attempt to strike him. I seemed to have hit home, and at once, with the mention of the name of Christ, this giant figure vanished, along with all his demons. Once while I was fasting, the cunning one even came as a monk, having the semblance of loaves of bread, and he offered me counsel, saying, 'Eat, and stop your many labors; you too are a man, and you are about to grow weak.' But perceiving his strategy, I rose to say my prayers, and he could not stand it, for he fled, and he had the appearance of smoke that passes through the door. How many times he presented the illusion of gold to me in the wilderness, in hopes that I would just touch and gaze on it! But I sang psalms in resistance to him, and he melted away. Many times he whipped me, and I said, 'Nothing *shall separate* me *from the love of Christ.*'[89] After that they lashed each other instead. But I was not the one who stopped them and nullified their actions—it was the Lord, who says, *I saw Satan fall like lightning from heaven.*[90] And,

my children, mindful of the Apostle's word, *I have applied all this to myself*,[91] so that you might learn not to falter in the discipline, nor to fear the devil and the apparitions of his demons.

41. "And since I have become a fool in describing these events, receive this as well for your protection and fearlessness, and trust me, for I am not lying. Once someone knocked at the door of my cell. And when I went out, I saw someone who seemed massive and tall. When I asked, 'Who are you?' he said, 'I am Satan.' I said, 'What are you doing here?' And he asked, 'Why do the monks and all the other Christians censure me without cause? Why do they curse me every hour?' When I replied, 'Why do you torment them?' he said, 'I am not the one tormenting them, but they disturb themselves, for I have become weak. Haven't they read that *the swords of the enemy have failed utterly, and that you have destroyed their cities?*[92] I no longer have a place—no weapon, no city. There are Christians everywhere, and even the desert has filled with monks. Let them watch after themselves and stop censuring me for no reason!' Marveling then at the grace of the Lord, I said to him: 'Even though you are always a liar, and never tell the truth, nevertheless this time, even if you did not intend to, you have spoken truly. For Christ in his coming reduced you to weakness, and after throwing you down he left you defenseless.' Upon hearing the Savior's name, and being unable to endure the scorching from it, he became invisible.

42. "Now if even the devil himself confesses that he is able to do nothing, then we ought to treat him and his demons with utter contempt. For his part, the enemy with his dogs has treacheries of the sort I have described, but we are able to scorn them, having learned of their weakness. Therefore let us not be plunged into despair in this way,

nor contemplate horrors in the soul, nor invent fears for ourselves, saying, 'How I hope that when a demon comes, he will not overthrow me—or pick me up and throw me down—or suddenly set himself next to me and cast me into confusion!' We must not entertain these thoughts at all, nor grieve like those who are perishing. Instead, let us take courage and let us always rejoice, like those who are being redeemed. And let us consider in our soul that the Lord is with us, he who routed them and reduced them to idleness. Let us likewise always understand and take it to heart that while the Lord is with us, the enemies will do nothing to us. For when they come, their actions correspond to the condition in which they find us; they pattern their phantasms after our thoughts. Should they find us frightened and distressed, immediately they attack like robbers, having found the place unprotected. Whatever we are turning over in our minds, this—and more—is what they do. For if they see that we are fearful and terrified, they increase even more what is dreadful in the apparitions and threats, and the suffering soul is punished with these. However, should they discover us rejoicing in the Lord, thinking about the good things to come, contemplating things that have to do with the Lord, reflecting that all things are in the hand of the Lord, and that a demon has no strength against a Christian, nor has he any authority over anyone—then seeing the soul safeguarded by such thoughts, they are put to shame and turned away. It was for this reason that the enemy, seeing Job so defended, departed from him, but finding Judas unarmed with these, took him captive. So if we wish to despise the enemy, let us always contemplate the things that have to do with the Lord, and let the soul always rejoice in hope. Then we shall see the antics of the demons to be like smoke, and we shall see them in flight rather than pursuit. For, as I said earlier, they are very cowardly, always expectant of the fire that has been prepared for them.

43. "For your fearlessness against them you have for yourselves also this sure sign. Whenever some apparition occurs, do not collapse in terror, but whatever it may be, ask first, bravely, 'Who are you and where do you come from?' And if it is a vision of holy ones, they will give you full assurance and transform your fear into joy. But if it is someone diabolical, it immediately is weakened, finding your spirit formidable. For simply by asking, 'Who are you and where do you come from?' you give evidence of your calmness. So when the son of Nun asked, he learned;[93] and the enemy did not go unseen when Daniel questioned him."[94]

44. All rejoiced while Antony talked about these things. In some, the love of virtue increased, in others carelessness was discarded, and in still others conceit was brought to an end. And all were persuaded to hate the demonic conniving, marveling at the grace given by the Lord to Antony for the discernment of spirits. So their cells in the hills were like tents filled with divine choirs—people chanting, studying, fasting, praying, rejoicing in the hope of future boons, working for the distribution of alms, and maintaining both love and harmony among themselves. It was as if one truly looked on a land all its own—a land of devotion and righteousness. For neither perpetrator nor victim of injustice was there, nor complaint of a tax collector.[95] And there was a multitude of ascetics, but among them all there was one mind, and it was set on virtue, so that when one saw the cells again, and such orderliness among the monks, he was moved to exclaim and say, *How lovely are your dwellings, Jacob, and your tents, Israel; like shady*

groves, and like a garden *by a river, and like tents which* the *Lord pitched, and like cedars beside the waters.*[96]

45. Then Antony, withdrawing by himself, as was his custom, to his own cell, intensified his discipline and sighed daily, reflecting on the dwellings in heaven, both longing for these and contemplating the ephemeral life of human beings. For also when he was about to eat or sleep or to attend to the other bodily necessities, he was ashamed as he thought about the intellectual part of the soul. Frequently when he was about to have a meal in the company of many other monks, recalling the spiritual food, he would excuse himself and go some distance from them, thinking he would blush if he were seen eating by others. He ate by himself, of course, according to his body's need, yet often with the brothers as well, doing this out of respect for them and becoming bold in the words he spoke for their assistance. He used to say that we ought to devote all our time to the soul instead of the body. He urged us to concede a little time to the body, out of necessity, but to be intent, for the most part, on the soul and to seek its benefit, so that it would not be dragged down by bodily pleasures, but rather that the body might be subservient to the soul. For this is what was said by the Savior: *Do not be anxious for your life, what you shall eat, nor about your body, what you shall put on.... And do not seek what you are to eat and what you are to drink, nor be of anxious mind. For all the nations of the world seek these things; and your Father knows that you need them. Instead, seek his Kingdom, and these things shall be yours as well.*[97]

46. After this, the persecution that then occurred under Maximin oppressed the Church,[98] and when the holy martyrs were led into Alexandria, he also left his cell and followed saying, "Let us go also, that we may enter the

going to Alex.

combat, or look upon those who do." He yearned to suffer martyrdom, but because he did not wish to hand himself over,[99] he rendered service to the confessors both in the mines and in the prisons. In the law court, he showed great enthusiasm, stirring to readiness those who were called forth as contestants, and receiving them as they underwent martyrdom and remaining in their company until they were perfected.[100] When the judge saw the fearlessness of Antony and of those with him, he issued the order that none of the monks were to appear in the law court, nor were they to stay in the city at all. All the others thought it wise to go into hiding that day, but Antony took this so seriously as to wash his upper garment and to stand in the next day in a prominent place in front, and to be clearly visible to the prefect. When, while all marveled at this, the prefect, passing by with his escort, saw him, he stood there calmly, demonstrating the purposefulness that belongs to us Christians. For, as I said before, he also prayed for martyrdom. He seemed, therefore, like one who grieved because he had not been martyred, but the Lord was protecting him to benefit us and others, so that he might be a teacher to many in the discipline that he had learned from the Scriptures. For simply by seeing his conduct, many aspired to become imitators of his way of life. Again, therefore, he served the confessors in his usual manner, and like one who had been bound along with them, he was one suffering in those ministrations.

47. When finally the persecution ended, and Peter the blessed bishop had made his witness,[101] Antony departed and withdrew once again to the cell, and was there daily being martyred by his conscience, and doing battle in the contests of the faith. He subjected himself to an even greater and more strenuous asceticism, for he was always fasting, and he had clothing with hair on the interior and skin

on the exterior that he kept until he died. He neither
bathed his body with water for cleanliness, nor did he
wash his feet at all, and he would not even consent to putting them in water unless it was necessary. Neither did
anyone ever see him undressed—indeed, no one saw the
body of Antony naked, except when he died and was
buried.

48. Now when he withdrew and decided to spend a
time in which he neither went out nor received any visitor,
a certain military officer named Martinianus became a nui-
sance to Antony. He had a daughter who was disturbed by
a demon, so that he stayed a long while, rapping on the
door and asking him to come out and to pray to God on his
daughter's behalf. He was unwilling to open the door, but
stooping from above said, "Why do you cry out to me,
man? I too am a man like you, but if you believe in Christ,
whom I serve, go, and in the same way you believe, pray to
God, and it will come to pass." Immediately he departed,
believing and calling on Christ, and having his daughter
purified of the demon. Through Antony many other
things have been done by the Lord, who says, *Ask, and it
will be given you.*[102] For though he did not open the door,
great numbers of those who suffered simply spent nights
outside his cell, and were cleansed when they believed and
prayed with sincerity.

49. But when he saw that he was disturbed by many
people and was not allowed to retire as he intended and
wished, apprehensive that, because of the things the Lord
was doing through him, either he might become prideful
or someone else might think more of him than was war-
ranted, he considered carefully and struck out, departing
into the upper Thebaid, in the direction of people who did
not know him.[103] And receiving bread from the brothers,
he sat by the banks of the river, looking to see if a boat

would come by, so that boarding it he might leave with them. While he watched for this, a certain voice came to him from above, saying, "Antony, where are you going, and why?" He was not distressed, but since he was accustomed to being called this way often, after he listened he answered, saying, "Since the crowds will not allow me to be alone, I want to go into the upper Thebaid because of the many annoyances of those who beset me here, and especially because they ask me for things that are beyond my power." But the voice said to him, "Even if you go into the Thebaid, and even if, as you are contemplating, you go down to the pastures,[104] you will have more, even twice as much, toil to endure. If you truly desire to be alone, go now into the inner mountain."[105] Antony said, "And who will show me the way? I have no knowledge of that." And immediately there were shown to him Saracens who were about to travel that route. Approaching them and drawing close, Antony asked to travel with them into the desert. And as if by the command of Providence, they eagerly welcomed him. After journeying three days and three nights in their company, he came to a very high hill. Below the hill there was water—perfectly clear, sweet and quite cold, and beyond there were plains, and a few untended date palms.

50. Then Antony, as if stirred by God, fell in love with the place, for this was the place the one who had spoken with him at the river bank had designated. Then, after first receiving loaves from his traveling companions, he remained on the mountain alone, no one else living with him. Looking on it as his own home, from that point forward he stayed in that place. Even the Saracens themselves, perceiving the zeal of Antony, would make it a point to travel that way and would joyfully bring loaves to him; but he also had a little modest relief from the date

Whoa, Tony.
Excessive oaths.

palms. In time, when the brothers learned of the place, they were anxious to send things to him, like children remembering a father. But Antony, seeing that some there were burdened and suffered hardship on account of the bread, and being considerate for the monks in this matter, took counsel with himself and asked some of those who came to him to bring him a hoe, an axe, and a little grain. When he gathered these things he inspected the land around the mountain, and finding a small, suitable place he plowed it; and having abundant water from the spring, he planted it. And by doing this every year, he had bread from then on, rejoicing because he would be annoying no one because of this, and because he kept himself from being a burden in all things. But after this, again seeing certain people coming, he also planted a few vegetables in order that the visitor might have a little relief from the rigor of that hard trip. At first, however, when the beasts in the wilderness came for water, they often would damage his crop and his planting. But gently capturing one of the beasts, he said to all of them, "Why do you hurt me, when I do you no injury? Leave, and in the name of the Lord do not come near here any longer." From then on, as if being afraid of the command, they did not come near the place.

Animals heed his command

51. So he was alone in the inner mountain devoting himself to prayers and the discipline. And the brothers who served him asked him if when they came every month they might bring him olives and pulse and oil, for he was at this point an old man. Furthermore, we know from those who visited him how many wrestlings he endured while dwelling there, *not against blood and flesh,* but against destructive demons.[106] For there they heard tumults and many voices, and crashing noises like the sound of weapons; and at night they saw the mountain filled with beasts. But they also observed him struggling as if against things

visible, and praying against them; and he encouraged the ones who came to him, while at the same time he fought, kneeling and praying to the Lord. And it was truly amazing that being alone in such a desert he was neither distracted by the demons who confronted him, nor was he frightened of their ferocity when so many four-legged beasts and reptiles were there. But truly he was one who, as Scripture says, having *trusted in the Lord*, was *like Mount Sion*,[107] keeping his mind unshaken and unruffled; so instead the demons fled and the wild beasts, as it is written, made peace with him.[108]

52. Then the devil watched Antony closely, and (as David sings) gnashed his teeth against him. But Antony was comforted by the Savior, remaining unaffected by his treacheries and various ploys. He sent beasts against him in the night as he lay sleepless; and nearly all the hyenas in that wilderness, emerging from their dens, surrounded him, and he was trapped in their midst. But as each one opened his mouth and threatened to bite, he, acquainted with the ways of the enemy, said to them all, "If you have received authority over me, I am prepared to be devoured by you. But if you were sent by demons, waste no time in retreating, for I am a servant of Christ." When Antony spoke these words they fled, being driven away by the remark as by a whip.

53. Then after a few days, as he was working (for he was also diligent in his labor), someone standing at the door pulled the strand that extended from his work, for he was weaving baskets, and these he gave to those who came to him in exchange for the things they brought to him. And rising he saw a beast resembling a man as far as the thigh, and having legs and feet like those of an ass. But Antony merely signed himself and said, "I am a servant of Christ. If you have been sent out against me—look, here I

am!" But the beast with his demons fled with such haste that he fell and died. And the death of the beast was the downfall of the demons, for they were eager to do everything to drive him from the wilderness, and they were powerless to do so.

54. One time the monks requested that he return to them, and oversee them and their places for a short time. He traveled with the monks who had come up to him, and a camel carried their loaves and water—for that whole desert is arid, and there is no water except in that mountain where his cell is, and they drew their water there. Now when the heat became oppressive and the water ran out along the way, they all were in peril. Having gone around to several places and finding no water, they were unable to travel any farther, but lay instead on the ground, and released the camel, despairing for their lives. But the old man, seeing everyone in peril, being greatly distressed and sighing deeply, departed from them a short distance. And bending his knees and stretching out his hands, he offered a prayer. Immediately the Lord made water gush forth from where he was praying. And after everyone drank his fill, they were revived. As soon as they had filled their waterskins they went out looking for the camel and found it, for it happened that the rope was coiled around a certain rock and so was held fast. After leading it back and watering it, they put the waterskins on the camel's back and completed the trip without incident. When he arrived at the outer cells, everyone who saw him embraced him as a father. And as if bringing provisions from the mountain, he entertained them with his words, and lent his assistance. Once again there was joy in the mountains, and zeal for progress, along with the encouragement due to their common faith. He too rejoiced then, both seeing the ardor of the monks and seeing also that his sister had grown old

preserving the life of virginity, and herself guided other virgins.

55. After a few days he returned once more to the mountain, and thereafter many visited him, and some who suffered were bold enough to approach him. For all the monks who came to him he unfailingly had the same message: to have faith in the Lord and love him; to guard themselves from lewd thoughts and pleasures of the flesh, and as it is written in Proverbs, not to be *deceived by the feeding of the belly;*[109] to flee vanity, and to pray constantly; to sing holy songs before sleep and after, and to take to heart the precepts in the Scriptures; to keep in mind the deeds of the saints, so that the soul, ever mindful of the commandments, might be educated by their ardor. But he especially urged them to practice constantly the word of the Apostle, *Do not let the sun go down on your anger,*[110] and to consider that this had been spoken with every commandment in mind—so that the sun should set neither on anger nor on any other sin of ours. He continued: "For it is good, even urgent, that the sun should not condemn us for an evil of the day, nor the moon for a sin, or even for an inclination, of the night. That this might be preserved in us, it is good to hear and obey the Apostle, for he says, 'Examine yourselves and test yourselves.'[111] Now daily let each one recount to himself his actions of the day and night, and if he sinned, let him stop. But if he has not sinned, let him avoid boasting; rather, let him persist in the good, and not become careless, nor condemnatory of a neighbor, nor declare himself righteous *until,* as the blessed apostle Paul said, *the Lord comes who* searches out *the hidden things.*[112] For frequently we are unaware of the things we do, but even though we do not recognize them, the Lord comprehends all things. Therefore, yielding the judgment to him, let us treat each other with compassion, and let us bear one an-

other's burdens.[113] Let us examine ourselves, however, and those things we are lacking let us hurry to complete. And may this remark serve as a precaution so that we might not sin: Let each one of us note and record our actions and the stirrings of our souls as though we were going to give an account to each other. And you can be sure that, being particularly ashamed to have them made known, we would stop sinning and even meditating on something evil. For who wants to be seen sinning? Or who, after sinning, would not prefer to lie, wanting it to remain unknown? So then, just as we would not practice fornication if we were observing each other directly, so also we will doubtless keep ourselves from impure thoughts, ashamed to have them known, if we record our thoughts as if reporting them to each other. Let this record replace the eyes of our fellow ascetics, so that, blushing as much to write as to be seen, we might never be absorbed by evil things. Patterning ourselves in this way, we shall be able to enslave the body,[114] as well as please the Lord and trample on the deceptions of the enemy."

56. These things he taught the ones he encountered. And with those who suffered he sympathized and prayed—and frequently the Lord heard the prayers he offered on behalf of many people. And Antony was neither boastful when he was heeded, nor disgruntled when he was not; rather, he gave thanks to the Lord always. He encouraged those who suffered to have patience and to know that healing belonged neither to him nor to men at all, but only to God who acts whenever he wishes and for whomever he wills. The ones who suffered therefore received the words of the old man as healing, and learned not to dwell on their infirmities but to be patient. And the ones who were cured were taught not to give thanks to Antony, but to God alone.

57. There happened to be a man named Fronto, from Palatium, and he suffered from a terrible condition, for he both bit his own tongue and was about to lose his eyes. When he came to the mountain, he pleaded with Antony to pray for him. Having done this, he said to Fronto, "Leave, and you will be healed." But when he grew worse and remained there for several days, Antony persisted in saying, "You will not be able to be healed while staying here. Go out, and when you arrive in Egypt you will see the sign accomplished in you." The man, having faith, went out, and as soon as he saw Egypt, his suffering ended and he became healthy, in accordance with the word that Antony learned from the Savior while praying.

58. A certain young woman from Busiris in Tripoli had a terrible and altogether hideous ailment—for when her tears along with the mucus and discharge from her ears fell to the ground, they immediately turned into worms. In addition, her body was paralyzed and her eyes were defective. The parents of this girl, learning about monks who went out to Antony, and having faith in the Lord who had healed the woman troubled with an issue of blood,[115] pleaded to travel with them, taking their daughter, and they consented. The parents, with their child, stayed outside the mountain with Paphnutius, the confessor and monk.[116] But the rest went in, and just when they wished to tell him about the young woman, he began to speak to them, describing the child's ailment and how she had traveled with them. And yet when they asked that these people be allowed to come to him, he would not allow this, but replied, "Go away, and you will find that she has been healed, unless she is dead. For this good deed is not mine, that she should come to me, a pitiable man; rather, her healing is from the Savior who works his mercy everywhere for those who call on him. So also in this case the

Lord has granted her prayer and his benevolence has shown me that he will cure the ailment of the child where she is." And indeed the wonder took place, and going out they found the parents exulting and the child completely healthy.

59. Once when two of the brothers were coming to him and they ran out of water along the way, one died and the other was very near the point of death. No longer having stamina to travel, the one surviving sat down on the ground, waiting to die. But Antony, sitting in the mountain, summoned two monks (for these happened to be there) and implored them, saying, "Take a jar of water and run on the road to Egypt. For of the two men who were coming, one has just now lost his life, and the other soon will, if you do not hurry. For a moment ago while praying this was revealed to me." And so when the monks went, they found one lying dead, and they buried him. The other they revived with water, and carried him back to the old man, for the distance was a full day's journey. But if anyone should raise a question about why he had not spoken out before the first had lost his life, in doing this he does not frame the inquiry correctly. For surely the judgment of death was not from Antony, but from God, who both passed judgment on the one, and sent the vision concerning the other. Now this marvel occurred only to Antony, for while sitting in the mountain, he kept his heart alert, and the Lord showed him distant happenings.

60. On another occasion he was sitting in the mountain, and looking up he saw someone being led up into the air, and great joy emanating from those who met him. Filled with wonder, and blessing such a great chorus, he prayed to learn what this might mean. And immediately a voice came to him, telling him that this was the soul of Amun, the monk in Nitria.[117] He had persevered in the

discipline until old age. Now the distance from Nitria to the mountain where Antony was equals a thirteen-day journey. Therefore the ones with Antony, seeing the old man in wonderment, asked to learn the reason; and they heard that Amun had just died. Because he had visited there quite often, he was well known, and many signs had taken place through him. One of those was this. One time when he had to cross the river called Lycus (it was flooded with water on that occasion), he asked the person with him, Theodore, to remain at a distance from him so that they would not see each other's nakedness while they swam through the water. Then, even after Theodore had departed, he was ashamed over seeing himself naked. All this time he felt disgrace and anxiety. Then suddenly he was transported to the opposite shore. When Theodore, a devout man himself, approached and saw that he had arrived before him and was not even moist from the water, he asked to learn how he crossed over. Seeing that he did not want to speak to him, he grabbed Amun's feet and threatened not to set him free until he learned from him what had happened. Seeing the contentiousness of Theodore, especially in the declaration he made, Amun exacted a pledge that he would tell no one of this until after his death. And then he explained that he had been lifted up and placed on the opposite shore, and that he had not walked on the water (for this was by no means possible for men, but only for the Lord, and for those whom he permits, as he had done in the case of the great apostle Peter). So after the death of Amun, Theodore related this.

But the monks to whom Antony spoke concerning the death of Amun made a note of the date, and when the brothers from Nitria came thirteen days later, they inquired and found out that Amun had died on the very day and hour in which the old man saw his soul being carried up. Both they and the others were astounded by the purity of Antony's soul—that he had learned instantaneously what had happened at a distance of thirteen-days' journey, and that he had seen the soul being led upward.

61. Still another time Archelaus, the count, having found him on the outside of the mountain, asked him simply to pray for Polycratia, the wonderful and Christ-inspired maiden of Laodicea. From overmuch stringency of discipline she was subject to great pains of the stomach and side, and her entire body had grown weak. So Antony prayed, and the count marked the day on which the prayer was spoken. Departing to Laodicea, he found the maiden in good health. When he inquired when and on what day she had been freed from the weakness, he pulled out the sheet on which he had marked the time of prayer. And checking it, he at once showed the writing on the paper, and everyone was astonished to realize that the Lord had freed her from her pains just when Antony was praying and appealing on her behalf to the goodness of the Savior.

62. With regard to the ones who visited him, he often predicted days in advance—and at times even months—the reason why they were coming. In fact, some came just to see him, and some because of sickness, and others because they suffered from demons. And all considered the effort of the journey neither an annoyance nor a loss, for each one went home feeling the benefit. And even though he said and saw such things, he asked that no one marvel at him on this account, but rather that they marvel at the Lord, for he has shown favor to us in the measure of our capacity for knowing him.

63. Having come down to the outer cells another time, and being asked to enter a boat and to pray with the monks, he alone sensed a horrible and extremely pungent odor. Now those in the boat said there were fish and dried

meat in the boat, and that the odor came from these, but he asserted that the stench was from something else. And even while he was speaking, a certain demon-possessed young man who, entering earlier, had hidden himself in the boat, suddenly cried out. But being rebuked in the name of our Lord Jesus Christ, the demon departed and the man was restored to health. Then everyone recognized that the stench was from the demon.

stinky demon

64. And someone else, a person of nobility, came to him afflicted by a demon. That demon was so hideous that the man affected by him did not know that he was going to Antony; his state was such that he used to devour his bodily excrement. The ones who brought him begged Antony to pray for him. And Antony, having compassion for the young man, offered prayers and stayed up with him the whole night. Then as dawn approached, the young man, suddenly jumping on Antony, shoved him. Though the ones who had accompanied him were furious at him, Antony said: "Do not be angry with the young man, for he is not responsible, but the demon in him. And because of his censure and his banishment to arid places, he raged and he did this. So glorify the Lord, for in this way his assault on me has become a sign of the demon's departure." When Antony had said this, immediately the young man was well. And finally coming to his senses, he realized where he was and embraced the old man, all the while giving thanks to God.

Calling out demons

65. About him a great number of the monks have told many other such things that came to pass through him— and their accounts are harmonious and consistent. And yet these do not seem so marvelous as the other still more wonderful things. Once when he was about to eat, rising to pray around the ninth hour, he felt himself being carried off in thought, and the wonder was that while standing

Arians in Alexandria cc 65-70

there he saw himself, as if he were outside himself, and as if he were being led through the air by certain beings. Next he saw some foul and terrible figures standing in the air, intent on holding him back so he could not pass by. When his guides combatted them, they demanded to know the reason, if he was not answerable to them. And when they sought an accounting of his life from the time of his birth, Antony's guides prevented it, saying to them, "The Lord has wiped clean the items dating from his birth, but from the time he became a monk, and devoted himself to God, you can take an account." Then as they leveled accusations and failed to prove them, the passage opened before him free and unobstructed. And just then he saw himself appear to come and stand with himself, and once more he was Antony, as before.

One time, forgetting to eat, he spent the remainder of the day and the entire night groaning and praying. For he was amazed to see how many foes our wrestling involves, and how many labors someone has in passing through the air, and he recalled that this is what the Apostle said, *following the prince of the power of the air.*[118] For in this sphere the enemy holds sway by doing battle and by attempting to stop those who are passing through. This is the reason he especially exhorted us: *Take the whole armor of God, that you may be able to withstand in the evil day. . . . that an opponent may be put to shame, having nothing evil to say of us.*[119] And having learned this, let us remember the Apostle's saying: *whether in the body or out of the body I do not know, God knows.*[120] Paul was *caught up to the third heaven,* and hearing *things that cannot be told*[121] he returned, whereas Antony saw himself entering the air and struggling until he became free.

66. He possessed this spiritual favor as well. When he sat alone on the mountain, if it ever happened that he was

puzzled, seeking some solution for himself, this was revealed to him by Providence as he prayed. He was the blessed one becoming, as it is written, *taught by God.*[122] Later, when once he had a conversation with someone who visited him about the soul's passage, and its location after this life, the next night someone called to him from above, saying, "Antony, get up—go out and look!" Going out, therefore (for he knew whom he would benefit from obeying), and looking up he saw someone huge, and ugly and fearsome, standing and reaching to the clouds—and certain beings ascending as if they had wings. And the huge figure extended his hands, and some were being held back by him, but others, flying upwards and finally passing him by, ascended without anxiety. That great one gnashed his teeth over those latter, but over those who fell back he rejoiced. And immediately a voice came to Antony: "Understand what you have seen!" And his understanding was opened, and he comprehended that it was the passage of the souls, and that the huge figure was the enemy who envies the faithful. And he perceived that he seizes and prevents the passing of those who are under his authority, but he is incapable of seizing, as they pass upwards, those who did not submit to him. Having seen this, then, and being prompted to recollection, he was striving more each day to advance *to what lies ahead.*[123] These things he did not report voluntarily, for he had spent much time in prayer and marveled at them privately, but when those with him inquired and pressed him, he was compelled to speak, being incapable, as a father, of concealing things from the children. On the contrary, he supposed his conscience to be pure, and that the accounts were to their advantage, since they would learn that the discipline yields good fruit, and that the visions frequently take place as an assuagement of the trials.

67. Furthermore, ,he was tolerant in disposition and

humble of soul. Though the sort of man he was, he honored the rule of the Church with extreme care, and he wanted every cleric to be held in higher regard than himself. He felt no shame at bowing the head to the bishops and priests; if even a deacon came to him for assistance, he discussed the things that are beneficial, and gave place to him in prayer, not being embarrassed to put himself in a position to learn. For indeed, often he would raise questions and ask to hear from those with him. And he acknowledged that he was helped if someone said anything useful. His face had a great and marvelous grace, and this spiritual favor he had from the Savior—for if he was present with a great number of monks, and someone who had not formerly met him wished to see him, immediately on arriving, he would pass by the others and run to him, as though drawn by his eyes. It was not his physical dimensions that distinguished him from the rest, but the stability of character and the purity of the soul. His soul being free of confusion, he held his outer senses also undisturbed, so that from the soul's joy his face was cheerful as well, and from the movements of the body it was possible to sense and perceive the stable condition of the soul, as it is written, *When the heart rejoices, the countenance is cheerful; but when it is in sorrow, the countenance is sad.*[124] So Jacob realized that Laban was planning treachery, and said to his wives, *the face of your father is not the same toward me as it was yesterday and the day before.*[125] So Samuel recognized David, for he had eyes that brought joy, and teeth white as milk.[126] And so also was Antony recognized, for he was never troubled, his soul being calm, and he never looked gloomy, his mind being joyous.

68. In things having to do with belief, he was truly wonderful and orthodox. Perceiving their wickedness and apostasy from the outset, he never held communion with

the Meletian schismatics.[127] And neither toward the Manichaeans nor toward any other heretics did he profess friendship, except to the extent of urging the change to right belief, for he held and taught that friendship and association with them led to injury and destruction of the soul. So in the same way he abhorred the heresy of the Arians, and he ordered everyone neither to go near them nor to share their erroneous belief. Once when some of the Ariomaniacs came to him, sounding them out and learning that they were impious, he chased them from the mountain, saying that their doctrines were worse than serpents' poison.

69. On another occasion when the Arians falsely claimed that he held the same view as they, he was quite irritated and angry at them. Then, summoned both by the bishops and all the brothers, he came down from the mountain, and entering into Alexandria, he publicly renounced the Arians, saying that theirs was the last heresy and the forerunner of the Antichrist. He taught the people that the Son of God is not a creature, and that he did not come into existence from nonbeing, but rather that he is eternal Word and Wisdom from the essence of the Father. "So," he asserted, "it is sacrilegious to say 'there was when he was not' for the Word coexisted with the Father always.[128] Therefore you are to have no fellowship with the most ungodly Arians, for there is no *fellowship of light with darkness*.[129] You are God-fearing Christians, but they, in saying that the Son and Word of God the Father is a creature, differ in no way from the pagans, who *serve the creature rather than the Creator*.[130] Be assured that the whole creation itself is angered at them, because they number among the creatures the Creator and Lord of all, in whom all things were made."[131]

70. When they heard the heresy that contends against

82

Christ condemned by such a man, all the people rejoiced. And all in the city ran together to see Antony. Both Greeks and those among them who are called priests came to the Lord's house, saying "We ask to see the man of God"—for this is what everyone called him. And there also the Lord cleansed many people of demons through him, and cured those who were mentally impaired. Many Greeks asked only to touch the old man, believing they would be benefited. It is beyond doubt that as many became Christians in those few days as one would have seen in a year. In fact, though some thought that he was annoyed by the crowds, and for this reason turned everyone away from him, he was undisturbed and said, "These are no more numerous than those demons with whom we wrestle on the mountain."

71. When he was departing, and we were escorting him,[132] as we came to the gate a certain woman cried out behind us, "Wait, man of God! My daughter is terribly distressed by a demon. Stop, I beg you, so that I will not risk injury by running!" When the old man heard her, and was implored by us, he was willing to stop. As the woman drew near, the child was hurled to the ground, but when Antony prayed, calling on the name of Christ, the child was raised with health restored, the impure demon having left her. And the mother praised God and everyone gave thanks. And he too rejoiced as he set out for the mountain, which was his own home.

72. Antony was also extremely wise. It was a marvel that although he had not learned letters, he was a shrewd and intelligent man. For example, once two Greek philosphers visited him, thinking they would be able to put him to the test. He was in the outer mountain at the time, and knowing what the men were from their appearance, he went out to them and said through an interpreter, "Why

did you go to so much trouble, you philosophers, to visit a foolish man?" When they responded that he was not foolish, but quite wise, he said to them, "If you came to a foolish man, your toil is superfluous, but if you consider me wise, become as I am, for we must imitate what is good. If I had come to you I would have imitated you; but since you came to me, become as I am; for I am a Christian." In amazement they withdrew, for they saw that even demons feared Antony.

73. Later, others like them encountered him in the outer mountain, thinking they would subject him to ridicule because he had not learned letters. To them Antony said: "What do you say? Which is first—mind or letters? And which is the cause of which—the mind of the letters, or the letters of the mind?" After their reply that the mind is first, and an inventor of the letters, Antony said: "Now you see that in the person whose mind is sound there is no need for the letters." This amazed both those who were present and these visitors. They went away marveling because they had seen such understanding in an untrained man, for he did not have the wild demeanor of someone reared on a mountain and growing old there. Instead he was gracious and civil, and his speech was seasoned with divine salt, so that no one resented him—on the contrary, all who came to him rejoiced over him.

74. After this some others came, and they were from those among the Greeks who are considered wise. They asked from him an explanation of our faith in Christ, but when they attempted to construct syllogisms concerning the preaching of the divine cross, and sought to ridicule this, Antony paused for a moment, at first pitying them in their ignorance, and said (through an interpreter who expertly translated his remarks): "Which is better—to confess a cross, or to attribute acts of adultery and pederasty to

those whom you call gods? For that which is stated by us is a signal of courage, and evidence of disdain for death, while your doctrines have to do with incidents of lewdness. Again, which is preferable, to say that the Word of God was not changed, but remaining the same he assumed a human body for the salvation and benefit of mankind—so that sharing in the human birth he might enable mankind to share the divine and spiritual nature—or to make the divine very much like the irrational beings, and on these grounds worship four-footed creatures and reptiles and images of men? For these are the objects of worship for you who are wise! How dare you ridicule us for saying that Christ has appeared as a man, when you, separating the soul from heaven, say that it has wandered and fallen from the vault of the heavens into a body? I wish it were only into a human body, and not that it changed and is transformed into four-footed creatures and reptiles! Our faith declares the coming of Christ, which took place for the salvation of mankind, but you are deceived in your belief concerning an uncreated soul. For our part, we know the power and benevolence of providence—that this advent of Christ was not impossible for God.[133] You, on the other hand, asserting that the soul is an image of the mind,[134] attribute falls to it and circulate myths to the effect that it is changeable. Then you introduce the notion that because of the soul, the mind itself is changeable. For what holds true for the image necessarily holds true also for that of which it is the image. But when you think things of this sort about the mind, realize that you are also blaspheming the Father of the mind himself.

75. "And concerning the cross, what would you say is preferable: when a plot is introduced by evil men, to endure the cross and not to cower in fear before any form of death, or to relate myths about the wanderings of Osiris

and Isis, the plots of Typhon, and the flight of Kronos, and swallowings of children and murder of fathers?[135] For these are the things you count as wise! And how is it that while you scoff at the cross, you do not marvel at the resurrection? For those who told the one also wrote the other. Or why, since you remember the cross, are you silent about the dead who were raised and the blind who recovered their sight, and the paralytics who were cured, and the lepers who were cleansed, and the walking on the sea, and the other signs and wonders that demonstrate that Christ is no longer a man, but God? Actually you seem to me to do yourselves an injustice, and not to have read our Scriptures honestly. But do read them and see that the things Christ has done reveal him to be God, who appeared for the salvation of mankind.

76. "And tell us your own views. What would you say, though, concerning the irrational beings, except something senseless and very brutish? But if, as I hear, you wish to say that these things are told by you in the manner of myth, and you allegorize the rape of Persephone, referring it to the earth, and the lameness of Hephaestus to fire, and Hera to the air, and Apollos to the sun, and Artemis to the moon, and Poseidon to the sea, nonetheless you do not worship God himself—on the contrary, you serve the creature instead of the God who created all things. Perhaps it was because of the creation's beauty that you composed such tales. Nevertheless it is fitting for you to go only so far as to admire, not to deify, the things created, lest you render the honor due the maker to the things made. Otherwise, the time has come for you to transfer honor due the architect to the house he has made or that due the general to the soldier. Now tell us what you say to these things, so that we may know if the cross holds anything worthy of ridicule!"

77. When those men were perplexed and turned one way, then another, Antony smiled and said (again, through an interpreter), "These things have their proof from sight itself, but since you press hard with arguments for demonstrating proof, and since you possess that skill, you want us also not to worship God without demonstrated proof from arguments. First tell me how things are accurately known, especially knowledge about God—through demonstration of arguments, or through an act of faith? And which is prior—the faith through an act or the demonstration through arguments?" And when they replied that the faith through an act is earlier, and that this is the accurate knowledge, Antony said, "You answer well, for faith comes from the disposition of the soul, but dialectic is from the skill of those who construct it. Therefore, for those in whom the action through faith is present, the demonstration through arguments is unnecessary, or perhaps even useless. For what we perceive by faith you attempt to establish through arguments. And often you are unable even to articulate what we see; so it is clear that the action through faith is better and more secure than your sophistic conclusions.

78. "We Christians, then, do not possess the mystery in a wisdom of Greek reasonings, but in the power supplied to us by God through Jesus Christ. For evidence that the account is true, see now that although we have not learned letters, we believe in God, knowing through his works his providence over all things. And for evidence that our faith is effective, see now that we rely on the trust that is in Christ, but you rely upon sophistic word battles. Among you the apparitions of the idols are being abolished, but our faith is spreading everywhere. And you by your syllogisms and sophisms do not convert people from Christianity to Hellenism, but we, by teaching faith in Christ, strip you of superstition, since all recognize that

Christ is God, and Son of God. By your beautiful language you do not impede the teaching of Christ, but we, calling on the name of Christ crucified, chase away all the demons you fear as gods. And where the sign of the cross occurs, magic is weakened and sorcery has no effect.

79. "Tell us, then, where are your oracles now? Where are the incantations of the Egyptians? Where are the magicians' phantasms? When, except at the time the cross of Christ came, did all these things come to an end and lose their strength? Is it this cross, then, that is worthy of ridicule—or the things, instead, that have been nullified and proved weak by it? For this too is a wonder: Your religion was never persecuted, and in every city it is honored among men, and yet our doctrines flourish and increase beyond yours. Your views perish, though acclaimed and celebrated far and wide.[136] But the faith and teaching of Christ, ridiculed by you and persecuted frequently by rulers, has filled the world. For when did the knowledge of God shine with such brilliance? When did moderation and virtue of virginity so manifest itself? Or when was death so despised, if it was not when the cross of Christ came? No one doubts this when he sees the martyrs who despise death on account of Christ, and when he sees the Church's virgins because of Christ keeping their bodies pure and undefiled.

80. "These proofs are sufficient to demonstrate that only faith in Christ is authentic for worship of God. But look—you still disbelieve, seeking syllogisms from the statements. We do not prove, as our teacher said, *in plausible words of* Greek *wisdom;*[137] but we persuade by the faith that clearly precedes the argumentation from the statements. Look, there are some here suffering from demons (for there were some who came to him distressed by demons, and he said, bringing them into their midst)—you

cleanse them, either by your syllogisms, or by any skill or magic you might wish, summoning your idols! Or, if you are not able, end the war you wage with us, and behold the power of the cross of Christ!" And when he had said these things, he called on Christ and signed those who suffered with the sign of the cross a second and third time. Immediately the men stood and were sound, coming to their senses and giving thanks to the Lord. And those who were called philosophers marveled and were truly astonished at the man's wisdom and the wonder that took place. But Antony said, "Why do you marvel at this? It is not we who do it, but Christ, who does these things through those who believe in him. You believe too, then, and you will see that what we have is not skill with words, but faith through love that works for Christ. And if you possess this also you will no longer seek proofs through arguments, but will realize that faith in Christ is sufficient in itself." Such were Antony's words; and marveling at him they departed, embracing him and acknowledging that they had benefited from him.

81. Antony's fame spread even to rulers. When Constantine Augustus and his sons Constantius Augustus and Constans Augustus learned of these things, they wrote to him as to a father and begged to receive responses from him.[138] He did not, however, make a great deal of the writings, nor did he rejoice over the letters; rather, he was just as he had been before the emperor wrote to him. When the writings were brought to him, he called the monks and said, "Do not consider it marvelous if a ruler writes to us, for he is a man. Marvel, instead, that God wrote the law for mankind, and has spoken to us through his own Son."[139] He preferred not to receive the letters, saying that he did not know how to respond to such things. But urged on by the monks, on the grounds that the rulers were Christians,

and in order that they not take offense at being rebuffed, he permitted them to be read. And he wrote in response, acknowledging them for their worship of Christ, and he offered counsel on things pertaining to salvation—that is, not to count present realities as great, but rather to consider the coming judgment, and to recognize that Christ alone is true and eternal ruler. He implored them to be men of human concern, and to give attention to justice and to the poor. And they rejoiced in receiving his response. So he was held in affection by everyone, and all asked to have him as a father.

82. Being known, then, as such a man, and in this way answering those who sought him out, he returned once more to the inner mountain, and he maintained his customary discipline. Frequently while sitting or walking with those who visited him, he was struck dumb, as it is written in Daniel.[140] Some time later he would resume what he had been saying with the brothers in his company, and those with him were aware that he was seeing some spectacle. For frequently when he was in the mountain he saw even the things that took place in Egypt. And these he described to Serapion the bishop who was within and watching Antony as he was occupied with the vision.[141] Once while he sat working, he went into ecstasy, so to speak, and he groaned a great deal during the spectacle. Then turning to his companions after a while, he moaned as he trembled; and then he prayed and bending his knees he remained that way for a long time. When he rose the old man was weeping. Those with him now began to tremble, and greatly frightened, they begged to learn from him what it was. And they pressed him a great deal until, being forced, he spoke. And so with much groaning he said, "My children, it is better for you to die before the things in the vision take place." Again they importuned him, and he said

through his tears, "Wrath is about to overtake the Church, and she is about to be handed over to men who are like irrational beasts. For I saw the table of the Lord's house, and in a circle all around it stood mules kicking the things within, just like the kicking that might occur when beasts leap around rebelliously. Surely you knew," he said, "how I groaned, for I heard a voice saying, 'My altar shall be defiled.'" The old man said this, and two years later the current assault of the Arians began, and the seizure of the churches took place during which, forcefully taking the sacred vessels, they caused them to be carried off by pagans. They also rousted the pagans from their workshops and compelled them to congregate with them. And in their presence they did what they wanted on the table. We all came to understand then that the vision of these kicking mules had announced in advance to Antony what the Arians now do senselessly, like beasts. But when he saw this spectacle, he comforted his companions by saying, "Children, do not lose heart. For just as the Lord has been angry, so again he will heal. And the Church will again quickly regain her proper beauty and shine forth as before. You will see those who are persecuted restored, and impiety withdrawn once again to its own hiding places, while the holy faith declares itself openly everywhere with complete liberty. Only do not defile yourselves with the Arians, for that teaching is not from the apostles, but from the demons, and from their father, the devil; indeed, it is infertile, irrational, and incorrect in understanding, like the senselessness of mules."

83. Such were the words and deeds of Antony. And we must not be incredulous because wonders of this kind were done by a man. It is the promise of the Savior, who says: *If you have faith as a grain of mustard seed, you will say to this mountain, "Move from here to there," and it will move, and*

nothing will be impossible to you.[142] And again, *Truly, truly, I say to you, if you ask anything of the Father, he will give it to you.... Ask, and you will receive.*[143] He is also the one who says to his disciples and to all who believe in him: *Heal the sick ... cast out the demons. You received without paying, give without pay.*[144]

84. Antony did, in fact, heal without issuing commands, but by praying and calling on the name of Christ, so it was clear to all that it was not he who did this, but the Lord bringing his benevolence to effect through Antony and curing those who were afflicted. Only the prayer was Antony's, and the discipline for the sake of which he dwelled in the mountain, and he rejoiced in the contemplation of divine realities, but he was disconsolate at being annoyed by so many visitors and drawn to the outer mountain. For even all the judges requested that he descend from the mountain, for it was impossible for them to come there because of the litigants who followed them. They asked, though, that he might come and that they might just see him. Then he turned aside and declined the journey to them, but they persisted and even sent those who were in soldiers' custody, so that he might be moved to come down for their sake. Swayed then by necessity, and seeing these people lamenting, he went to the outer mountain. And on this occasion also his effort was not without benefit, for his arrival worked to the advantage and benefaction of many. He aided the judges, advising them to value justice over everything else, and to fear God, and to realize that by the judgment with which they judged, they themselves would be judged.[145] Nevertheless, he loved more than everything else his way of life in the mountain.

85. Another time he was subjected to this kind of pressure from people in need, and the military commander, through many messengers, asked him to come. And after

he came and delivered a few statements about salvation and remarks pertaining to those who required help, he hastened to return. When the one called the duke implored him to stay, he replied that it was impossible to spend time with them, and by a graceful illustration he persuaded the duke, saying, "Just as fish perish when they lie exposed for a while on the dry land, so also the monks relax their discipline when they linger and pass time with you. Therefore, we must rush back to the mountain, like the fish to the sea—so that we might not, by remaining among you, forget the things within us." Hearing these and many other words from him, and marveling, the commander said, "Truly, this man is a servant of God, for how could so great and substantial an intellect belong to a common man unless he were loved by God?"

86. There was one military commander—Balacius was his name—who sharply persecuted us Christians because of his enthusiasm for the despicable Arians. And since he was so savage as to beat virgins and to strip and flog monks, Antony sent to him, and the gist of the letter he wrote was this: "I see wrath coming upon you. Stop persecuting Christians, then, that the wrath may not overtake you—for even now it is coming upon you!" But Balacius, laughing, threw the letter to the ground, spitting on it, and he insulted those who brought it, instructing them to tell Antony this: "Since you are anxious about the monks, I shall now search you out also." Not even five days passed, and the wrath overtook him. For Balacius and Nestorius, the prefect of Egypt, were going to the first stopping place out from Alexandria, which is called Chaireu, and both were riding horses. The mounts were Balacius's own, and were the gentlest of all he had trained. But before they reached the place, they began to frisk with each other, as they do, and suddenly the gentler horse, which Nestorius

rode, bit Balacius, threw him down, and attacked him. And he tore his thigh with his teeth so badly that he was carried immediately back to the city, but within three days he died. And all were amazed that what Antony foretold was fulfilled so quickly.[146]

87. This is the way he warned those who were cruel. But the others who came to him he admonished in such a manner that they forgot their lawsuits and blessed those who withdrew from the life of the world. He lent his support to victims of injustice so avidly that it was possible to think that he, not the others, was the injured party. Again, he was so competent in bringing benefit to everyone that many in military service and many of the prosperous laid aside the burdens of life, and became monks from that point on. It was as if he were a physician given to Egypt by God. For who went to him grieving and did not return rejoicing? Who went in lamentation over his dead, and did not immediately put aside his sorrow? Who visited while angered and was not changed to affection? What poor person met him in exhaustion who did not, after hearing and seeing him, despise wealth and console himself in his poverty? What monk, coming to him in discouragement, did not become all the stronger? What young man, coming to the mountain and looking at Antony, did not at once renounce pleasures and love moderation? Who came to him tempted by a demon and did not gain relief? And who came to him distressed in his thoughts and did not find his mind calmed?

88. This too was great in Antony's asceticism—that possessing the gift of discerning spirits, as I said before, he recognized their movements and he knew that for which each one of them had a desire and appetite. Not only did he himself suffer no ridicule from them, but offering encouragement to those who were distressed in their thoughts, he

taught how they might overturn the demons' plots, describing the weaknesses and the treacheries of the ones who executed them. Each visitor, then, as if anointed for the contest by him, came down acting boldly against the strategies of the devil and his demons. And how many young women who had men hoping to marry them, on simply seeing Antony at a distance, remained virgins for Christ! And people came to him from foreign lands also, and having received help with all the others, they turned toward home as though sent on their way by a father. And indeed, now that he has died, they all, being bereft of a father, comfort one another solely by the memory of him, clinging to his admonitions and warnings.

89. It is worthwhile for me to recall, and for you to hear (as you wish) what the end of his life was like, for even his death has become something imitable.

He came, as he customarily did, to inspect the monks who resided in the outer mountain, and when he learned from providence about his death, he spoke to the brothers, saying: "This is the last visitation I shall make to you, and I wonder if we shall see each other again in this life. Now it is time for me to perish, for I am nearly a hundred and five years old." When they heard him, they wept and embraced and kissed the old man. But he, like one sailing from a foreign city to his own, talked cheerfully and exhorted them not to lose heart in their labors nor to grow weary in the discipline, but to live as though dying daily. He told them, "Be zealous in protecting the soul from foul thoughts, as I said before, and compete with the saints, but do not approach the Meletian schismatics, for you know their evil and profane reputation. Nor are you to have any fellowship with the Arians, for their impiety is evident to everyone. And should you see the judges advocating their cause, do not be troubled, for this will end—their fantacizing pos-

95

ture is something perishable and ephemeral. Rather, keep yourselves pure from contact with them and guard both the tradition of the fathers and especially the holy faith in our Lord Jesus Christ, which you have learned from the Scriptures and have often had recalled to you by me."

90. When the brothers pressed him to stay with them and die there, he refused for a number of reasons, as he indicated even while remaining silent, but because of one in particular. The Egyptians love to honor with burial rites and to wrap in linens the bodies of their worthy dead, and especially of the holy martyrs, not burying them in the earth, but placing them on low beds and keeping them with them inside, and they intend by this practice to honor the deceased.[147] Antony frequently asked a bishop to instruct the people on this matter, and he similarly corrected laymen and chastised women, saying, "It is neither lawful nor at all reverent to do this. The bodies of the patriarchs and the prophets are preserved even to this day in tombs, and the Lord's own body was put in a tomb, and a stone placed there hid it until he rose on the third day." And in saying these things he showed that the person violates the Law who does not, after death, bury the bodies of the deceased, even though they are holy. For what is greater or holier than the Lord's body? The many who heard him thereafter buried their dead, and gave thanks to the Lord that they had been taught well.

91. But Antony, aware of this practice and afraid that they might perform it for his body, pressed on, departing from the monks in the outer mountain. He entered the inner mountain to stay there as usual and in a few months became ill. He called those who were with him (they were two men who had also remained within, practicing the discipline fifteen years and assisting him on account of his age)[148] and said to them, "I am going the way of the fathers,

as it is written,[149] for I see myself being summoned by the
Lord. Be watchful and do not destroy your lengthy discipline, but as if you were making a beginning now, strive to
preserve your enthusiasm. You know the treacherous demons—you know how savage they are, even though weakened in strength. Therefore, do not fear them, but rather
draw inspiration from Christ always, and trust in him.
And live as though dying daily, paying heed to yourselves
and remembering what you heard from my preaching.
And let there be no fellowship between you and the schismatics, and certainly none with the heretical Arians. For
you know how I too have shunned them because of their
Christ-battling and heterodox teaching. Rather, strive always to be bound to each other as allies, first of all in the
Lord, and then in the saints, so that after death *they may receive you into the eternal habitations* as friends and companions.[150] Consider these things and turn your minds to
them, and if you care for me and remember me as a father,
do not permit anyone to take my body to Egypt, lest they
set it in the houses. It was for this reason that I went to the
mountain and came here. You know how I always corrected the ones who practiced this and ordered them to stop
that custom. Therefore, perform the rites for me yourselves, and bury my body in the earth. And let my word be
kept secret by you, so that no one knows the place but you
alone. For in the resurrection of the dead I shall receive my
body incorruptible once again from the Savior. Distribute
my clothing. To Bishop Athanasius give the one sheepskin
and the cloak on which I lie, which he gave to me new, but
I have by now worn out. And to Bishop Serapion give the
other sheepskin, and you keep the hair garment. And now
God preserve you, children, for Antony is leaving and is
with you no longer."

92. When he had said this, and they embraced him, he

lifted his feet, and as if seeing friends who had come to him and being cheered by them (for as he lay there, his face seemed bright), he died and was taken to the fathers. Then they, in accordance with the commands he had given them, making preparations and wrapping his body, buried it in the earth, and to this day no one knows where it has been hidden except those two. And each of those who received the blessed Antony's sheepskin, and the cloak worn out by him, keeps it safe like some great treasure. For even seeing these is like beholding Antony, and wearing them is like bearing his admonitions with joy.

93. This was the end of Antony's life in the body, and what we related above was the beginning of his discipline. Even if these things are slight in comparison with that man's virtue, yet you can deduce from them what kind of person the man of God, Antony, was, who kept his fervent commitment to the discipline from his youth to such an advanced age. He never succumbed, due to old age, to extravagance in food, nor did he change his mode of dress because of frailty of the body, nor even bathe his feet with water, and yet in every way he remained free of injury. For he possessed eyes undimmed and sound, and he saw clearly. He lost none of his teeth—they simply had been worn to the gums because of the old man's great age. He also retained health in his feet and hands, and generally he seemed brighter and of more energetic strength than those who make use of baths and a variety of foods and clothing.

Proof of his virtue and that his soul was loved by God is found in the fact that he is famous everywhere and is marveled at by everyone, and is dearly missed by people who never saw him. Neither from writings, nor from pagan wisdom, nor from some craft was Antony acclaimed, but on account of religion alone. That this was something given by God no one would deny. For how is it that he was heard of, though concealed and sitting in a mountain, in Spain and Gaul, and in Rome and Africa, unless it was the God who everywhere makes his men known who also promised this to Antony in the beginning? For even though they themselves act in secret, and may want to be forgotten, nevertheless the Lord shows them like lamps to everyone, so that those who hear may know that the commandments have power for amendment of life, and may gain zeal for the way of virtue.

94. Therefore, read these things now to the other brothers so that they may learn what the life of the monks ought to be, and so they may believe that our Lord and Savior Jesus Christ glorifies those who glorify him, and not only leads those who serve him to the end into the Kingdom of heaven, but even here, though they conceal themselves and seek to retire, he makes them known and celebrated everywhere, both because of their own virtue and because of their assistance to others. And if the need arises, read this to the pagans as well, so they may understand by this means that our Lord Jesus Christ is God and Son of God—and, additionally, that the Christians who are sincerely devoted to him and truly believe in him not only prove that the demons, whom the Greeks consider gods, are not gods, but also trample and chase them away as deceivers and corrupters of mankind, through Jesus Christ our Lord, to whom belongs glory forever and ever. Amen.

A Letter of Athanasius, Our Holy Father, Archbishop of Alexandria, to Marcellinus on the Interpretation of the Psalms

1. I marvel at your conduct in Christ, dear Marcellinus. Indeed you are successfully enduring the present trial, although you have suffered many tribulations in it, and you do not neglect the discipline.[1] For when I inquired from your letter-bearer how you fare in your continuing illness, I learned that you maintain a studious attitude toward all the holy Scripture, but that you read most frequently the Book of Psalms, and strive to comprehend the meaning contained in each psalm. On the basis of this, then, I commend you, since I too have a great fondness for the same book—just as I have for all the Scripture. Indeed, it so happens that I had a conversation with a learned old man, and I wish to write you those things that old master of the Psalter told me about it. For there is a certain grace and persuasiveness combined with the reasonable statement. He said this:

2. *All Scripture* of ours, my son—both ancient and new—is *inspired by God and profitable for teaching,* as it is written.[2] But the Book of Psalms possesses a certain winning exactitude for those who are prayerful. Each sacred book supplies and announces its own promise. The Pentateuch, for instance, relates the beginning of the world and

101

the deeds of the patriarchs, both the exodus of Israel out of Egypt and the decree of the legislation. The Triteuch[3] tells the possession of the land and the exploits of the judges, as well as David's ancestral line. The books of the Kings and Chronicles recount the stories of the rulers. And Esdras[4] describes the release from the captivity, the return of the people, and the construction of the temple and the city. The books of the Prophets contain foretellings about the sojourn of the Savior, admonitions concerning divine commands and reprimands against transgressors, as well as prophecies for the gentiles. Yet the Book of Psalms is like a garden containing things of all these kinds, and it sets them to music, but also exhibits things of its own that it gives in song along with them.

3. It sings the events of Genesis in Psalm 18: *The heavens declare the glory of God; and the firmament proclaims the work of his hands*, and in Psalm 23: *The earth is the Lord's and the fullness thereof; the world, and all that dwell in it. He has founded it upon the seas.* The themes of Exodus and Numbers and Deuteronomy it chants beautifully in Psalms 77 and 113 when it says: *At the going forth of Israel from Egypt, of the house of Jacob from a barbarous people, Judea became his sanctuary, and Israel his dominion.*[5] It hymns the same events in Psalm 104: *He sent forth Moses his servant, and Aaron whom he had chosen. He established among them his words, and his wonders in the land of Cham. He sent forth darkness, and made it dark; yet they rebelled against his words. He turned their waters into blood, and he destroyed their fish. Their land produced frogs abundantly, in the chambers of their kings. He spoke, and the dog-fly came, and lice into all their coasts.*[6] And it is possible to discover that this whole psalm generally and Psalm 105 were written concerning these same events. And matters pertaining to the priesthood and the tabernacle it proclaims in the "going out from the tabernacle"[7] in Psalm 28: *Bring to*

the Lord, you sons of God, bring to the Lord young rams; bring to the Lord glory and honor.

4. The things concerning Joshua and the judges it manifests somehow in the one hundred and sixth when it says: *And they establish for themselves cities of habitation, and they sow fields and plant vineyards.* For the land of the promise was given over to the people of Joshua. And when it says repeatedly in the same psalm, *Then they cried to the Lord in their affliction, and he delivered them from their distresses*, it signifies the Book of Judges. When they cry out, he raises judges in the right time and saves his people from their tribulations. The stories of the kings it sings, surely, in the nineteenth psalm, stating: *Some glory in chariots, and some in horses: But we will glory in the name of the Lord our God. They are overthrown and fallen: But we are risen, and have been set upright. O Lord, save the King, and hear us in whatever day we call upon you.* The events of Esdras in Psalm 125 (of the gradual psalms)[8] it sings: *When the Lord overturned the captivity of Sion, we became as comforted ones*, and again in 121: *I was glad when they said to me, Let us go into the house of the Lord. Our feet stood in your courts, O Jerusalem. Jerusalem is built as a city whose fellowship is complete. For to that place the tribes went up, the tribes of the Lord, as a testimony for Israel.*

5. The pronouncements of the Prophets are declared in nearly every psalm. About the visitation of the Savior, and that he will make his sojourn as one who is God, so it says in the forty-ninth psalm: *The Lord our God shall come manifestly, and shall not keep silence*, and in the one hundred and seventeenth: *Blessed is he that comes in the name of the Lord: We have blessed you out of the house of the Lord. God is Lord and he has shined upon us.* And that this one is the Word of the Father, so it sings in Psalm 106: *He sent his Word, and healed them, and delivered them out of their destructions.* The Coming One is God himself, and the Word who is sent. Be-

cause the Psalter knows that this Word is the Son of God, it chants the voice of the Father in the forty-fourth psalm: *My heart has uttered a good Word.* And again in Psalm 109: *I have begotten you from the womb before the morning.* What else would someone say the offspring of the Father is except his Word and his Wisdom? Because Scripture knew that it was this one to whom the Father said, *Let there be light, and firmament and all things,*[9] this book also contains the saying, *By the Word of the Lord the heavens were established; and all the host of them by the breath of his mouth.*[10]

6. It knew Christ himself as the Coming One and indeed it especially speaks concerning him in the forty-fourth psalm: *Your throne, O God, is forever and ever: The scepter of your Kingdom is a scepter of righteousness. You have loved righteousness and hated iniquity. Therefore God, your God, has anointed you with the oil of gladness beyond your fellows.* And lest someone suppose that he comes only in semblance, it makes clear that this same one will become man and that this is he through whom all things were made,[11] as it says in Psalm 86:[12] *Mother of Sion shall say, a man, and a man was begotten in her, and the Most High himself formed her.* This is tantamount to saying, *And the Word was God,* and *all things were made through him,* and *the Word became flesh.*[13] On this account also, since it knows that this was from a virgin, the Psalter was not silent, but immediately gives some clear expression in the forty-fourth psalm, saying, *Hear, O daughter, and see, and incline your ear; forget also your people and your father's house, because the King has desired your beauty.* Again, this is like that which is said by Gabriel, *Hail, O favored one, the Lord is with you!*[14] For indeed, having stated that he is Christ, soon thereafter it made known the human birth from the virgin in saying, *Hear, O daughter.*[15] Take note that Gabriel calls Mary by name, since he is dissimilar to her in terms of origination, but David the Psalmist proper-

ly addresses her as *daughter*, because she happened to be from his seed.

7. And having declared that he would become man, afterwards the Psalter also points to his passibility in the flesh. Perceiving, then, that there would be a plot on the part of the Jews, it sings in Psalm 2, *Wherefore did the heathen rage, and the nations imagine vain things? The kings of the earth stood up, and the rulers gathered themselves together against the Lord and against his Anointed.* In the twenty-first it tells the manner of the death from the Savior's own lips: ... *you have brought me down to the dust of death. For many dogs have surrounded me; the assembly of the wicked has attacked me on all sides. They pierced my hands and feet. They counted all my bones. They divided my garments among themselves, and cast lots upon my raiment.* When it speaks of the piercing of the hands and feet, what else than a cross does it signify? After teaching all these things, it adds that the Lord suffers these things not for his own sake, but for ours. And it says again through his own lips in Psalm 87, *Your wrath has pressed heavily upon me,* and in Psalm 68, *Then I restored that which I did not take away.* For although he was not himself obliged to give account for any crime, he died—but he suffered on our behalf, and he took on himself the wrath directed against us on account of the transgression, as it says in Isaiah, *He took on our weaknesses.*[16] This is evident also when we say in Psalm 137, *The Lord will recompense them on my behalf,*[17] and the Spirit says in the seventy-first, *and he will save the children of the needy, and shall bring low the false accuser ... for he has delivered the poor from the oppressor; and the laborer, who had no helper.*

8. On this account it foretells his bodily ascension into heaven, and says in Psalm 23, *Lift up your gates, you princes, and be lifted up, you everlasting doors, and the king of glory shall come in.* And in the forty-sixth, *God is gone up with a shout,*

the Lord with a sound of a trumpet. It announces the session at God's right hand, and says in Psalm 109, *The Lord said to my Lord, Sit on my right hand until I make your enemies your footstool*. And in the ninth psalm it shouts aloud the destruction of the devil that took place: *You sat on the throne, as one judging righteousness. You have rebuked the nations, and the ungodly one has perished*. It did not even conceal the fact that he received all the authority of judgment from the Father, but also announces that he is coming as judge of all in Psalm 71: *O God, give your judgment to the king, and your righteousness to the king's son, that he may judge your people with righteousness, and your poor with judgment*. And in the forty-ninth it says: *He shall summon the heaven above, and the earth, that he may judge his people.* . . . *And the heavens shall declare his righteousness, for God is judge*. And in the eighty-first we read: *God stands in the assembly of the gods; and in the midst of them he will judge gods*. Also one may learn from it about the calling of nations—in many psalms, but best in Psalm 46: *Clap your hands, all nations; shout to God with a voice of exultation*. Likewise in the seventy-first: *The Ethiopians shall fall down before him, and his enemies shall lick the dust. The kings of Tharsis, and the isles, shall bring presents. The kings of the Arabians and Sheba shall offer gifts. And all kings of the earth shall worship him; all the gentiles shall serve him*. These things are sung in the Psalms, and they are foretold in each of the other books of Scripture.

9. And not being ignorant, the old man then would say: In each book of Scripture the same things are specially declared. This report exists in all of them, and the same agreement of the Holy Spirit. Indeed, just as it is possible to discover in this book things in the others, so also things in this book are frequently found in the others. For Moses writes a hymn, and Isaiah is hymning, and Habakkuk prays with a hymn.[18] Furthermore, in each book one is

able to find prophecies and legislations and narratives. For the same Spirit is over all, and in each case in accordance with the distinction that belongs to it, each serves and fulfills the grace given to it, whether it is prophecy, or legislation, or the record of history, or the grace of the psalms. Since it is one and the same Spirit,[19] from whom are all distinctions, and it is indivisible by nature—because of this surely the whole is in each, and as determined by service the revelations and the distinctions of the Spirit pertain to all and to each severally. Furthermore, according to the reserved need, each frequently, when the Spirit takes over, serves the Word. Therefore, as I said previously, when Moses is legislating, sometimes he prophesies and sometimes sings, and the Prophets when they are prophesying sometimes issue commands, like *Wash yourselves, be clean. Cleanse your heart from wickedness, O Jerusalem,*[20] and sometimes recount history, as Daniel does the events surrounding Susanna[21] and Isaiah does referring to Rabshakeh and Sennacherib.[22] In this way the Book of Psalms, possessing the characteristic feature of the songs, itself chants those things in modulated voice that have been said in the other books in the form of detailed narrative, as already mentioned. And sometimes at least, it also legislates: *Cease from anger, and forsake wrath,*[23] and *Turn away from evil and do what is good; seek peace, and pursue it.*[24] And it narrates at times about the journeying of Israel, and prophesies concerning the Savior, as was said previously.

10. Let there be such a common grace of the Spirit in all, and let it be found existing in each one, the same grace among all, whenever the need demands and the Spirit desires. The more and the less in this need do not differ, as each unstintingly accomplishes and completes its own service. But even so, the Book of Psalms thus has a certain grace of its own, and a distinctive exactitude of expression.

For in addition to the other things in which it enjoys an affinity and fellowship with the other books, it possesses, beyond that, this marvel of its own—namely, that it contains even the emotions of each soul, and it has the changes and rectifications of these delineated and regulated in itself. Therefore anyone who wishes boundlessly to receive and understand from it, so as to mold himself, it is written there. For in the other books one hears only what one must do and what one must not do. And one listens to the Prophets so as solely to have knowledge of the coming of the Savior. One turns his attention to the histories, on the basis of which he can know the deeds of the kings and saints. But in the Book of Psalms, the one who hears, in addition to learning these things, also comprehends and is taught in it the emotions of the soul, and, consequently, on the basis of that which affects him and by which he is constrained, he also is enabled by this book to possess the image deriving from the words.[25] Therefore, through hearing, it teaches not only not to disregard passion, but also how one must heal passion through speaking and acting. Now there certainly are in the other books preventive words that forbid wickedness, but in this book is also prescribed how one must abstain.[26] Of such a sort is the commandment to repent—for to repent is to cease from sin. Herein is prescribed also how to repent and what one must say in the circumstances of repentance. Furthermore, the Apostle said, *Suffering produces endurance* in the soul, *and endurance produces character, and character produces hope, and hope does not disappoint us.*[27] In the Psalms it is written and inscribed how one must bear sufferings, what one must say to one suffering afflictions, what to say after afflictions, how each person is tested, and what the words of those who hope in God are. Furthermore, there is a command to give thanks in all circumstances,[28] but the Psalms also teach what one must say when giving thanks. Then hearing from others that as many as wish to live a godly life will be persecuted,[29] from these we are taught how one must call out while fleeing, and what words must be offered to God while being persecuted and after being delivered subsequent to persecution. We are asked to bless the Lord, and to acknowledge him. But in the Psalms we are instructed how one must praise the Lord and by speaking what words we properly confess our faith in him. And in the case of each person one would find the divine hymns appointed for us and our emotions and equanimity.

11. There is also this astonishing thing in the Psalms. In the other books, those who read what the holy ones say, and what they might say concerning certain people, are relating the things that were written about those earlier people. And likewise, those who listen consider themselves to be other than those about whom the passage speaks, so that they only come to the imitation of the deeds that are told to the extent that they marvel at them and desire to emulate them.[30] By contrast, however, he who takes up this book—the Psalter—goes through the prophecies about the Savior, as is customary in the other Scriptures, with admiration and adoration, but the other psalms he recognizes as being his own words. And the one who hears is deeply moved, as though he himself were speaking, and is affected by the words of the songs, as if they were his own songs. And for the sake of clarity of expression, do not hesitate, as the blessed Apostle says, to repeat the very things they say.[31] Most words belong to the patriarchs, and were spoken as their own. And Moses used to speak and God answered, and both Elijah and Elisha, situated on Mount Carmel, would call on the Lord, and they would say: *As the Lord lives, before whom I stand today.*[32] And the principal words of the holy Prophets are those concerning the Savior. There-

after a great number have to do with both the gentiles and Israel. Nevertheless no one would ever utter the words of the patriarchs as his own, nor would anyone dare to imitate and to say Moses' own words; those of Abraham about his slave and Ishmael, and the things concerning the great Isaac no one, even if the same need might perforce seize him, would boldly utter as his own. And if anyone should sympathize with those who suffer, and at some time should hold a desire for something better, he would never speak as Moses: *Reveal yourself to me!*[33] and again, *If you will forgive their sin, forgive it; and if you will not forgive, blot me out of your book which you have written.*[34] But neither would anyone, taking the books of the Prophets as his own words, blame or praise those doing things similar to these, whom the prophets blamed and praised. Nor would anyone imitate by uttering as if his own the saying, *As the Lord lives, before whom I stand today.* Indeed, it is clear that one who reads the books utters them not as his own words, but as the words of the saints and those who are signified by them. But contrariwise, remarkably, after the prophecies about the Savior and the nations, he who recites the Psalms is uttering the rest as his own words, and each sings them as if they were written concerning him, and he accepts them and recites them not as if another were speaking, nor as if speaking about someone else. But he handles them as if he is speaking about himself. And the things spoken are such that he lifts them up to God as himself acting and speaking them from himself. For not as in the case of the sayings of the patriarchs and Moses and the other Prophets will he be cautious of these things, but he who chants these will be especially confident in speaking what is written as if his own and about him. For the Psalms comprehend the one who observes the commandment as well as the one who transgresses, and the action of each. And it is necessary for everyone to be constrained by these, and either as a keeper of the law or as its transgressor, to speak the words that have been written about each.

12. And it seems to me that these words become like a mirror to the person singing them, so that he might perceive himself and the emotions of his soul, and thus affected, he might recite them. For in fact he who hears the one reading receives the song that is recited as being about him, and either, when he is convicted by his conscience,[35] being pierced, he will repent, or hearing of the hope that resides in God, and of the succor available to believers—how this kind of grace exists for him—he exults and begins to give thanks to God. Therefore, when someone sings the third psalm, recognizing his own tribulations, he considers the words in the psalm to be his own. And then when someone sings the eleventh and sixteenth he considers how he is one making announcement in reference to his own confidence and prayer, and in the fiftieth, how it is speaking the proper words of his own repentance. When someone sings the fifty-third, the fifty-fifth, the fifty-sixth, and the one hundred and forty-first, he considers not how someone else is persecuted, but how he, being the one who suffers, is affected. And these words, as his own, he chants to the Lord. And so, on the whole, each psalm is both spoken and composed by the Spirit so that in these same words, as was said earlier, the stirrings of our souls might be grasped, and all of them be said as concerning us, and the same issue from us as our own words, for a remembrance of the emotions in us, and a chastening of our life. For what those who chant have said, these things also can be examples and standards for us.

13. Again, the same grace is from the Savior, for when he became man for us he offered his own body in dying for our sake, in order that he might set all free from death.

And desiring to show us his own heavenly and well-pleasing life, he provided its type in himself, to the end that some might no more easily be deceived by the enemy, having a pledge for protection—namely, the victory he won over the devil for our sake. For this reason, indeed, he not only taught, but also accomplished what he taught, so that everyone might hear when he spoke, and seeing as in an image, receive from him the model for acting, hearing him say, *Learn from me, for I am gentle and lowly in heart.*[36] A more perfect instruction in virtue one could not find than that which the Lord typified in himself. For whether the issue is forbearance of evil, or love for mankind, or goodness, or courage, or compassion, or pursuit of justice, one will discover all present in him, so that nothing is lacking for virtue to one who considers closely this human life of his. Cognizant of this, Paul said, *Be imitators of me, as I am of Christ.*[37] Those legislators among the Greeks possess the grace as far as speaking goes, but the Lord, being true Lord of all and one concerned for all, performed righteous acts, and not only made laws but offered himself as a model for those who wish to know the power of acting. It was indeed for this reason that he made this resound in the Psalms before his sojourn in our midst, so that just as he provided the model of the earthly and heavenly man in his own person, so also from the Psalms he who wants to do so can learn the emotions and dispositions of the souls, finding in them also the therapy and correction suited for each emotion.

14. If the point needs to be put more forcefully, let us say that the entire Holy Scripture is a teacher of virtues and of the truths of faith, while the Book of Psalms possesses somehow the perfect image for the souls' course of life. For as one who comes into the presence of a king assumes a certain attitude, both of posture and expression, lest speaking differently he be thrown out as boorish, so

also to the one who is running the race of virtue and wishes to know the life of the Savior in the body the sacred book first calls to mind the emotions of the soul through the reading, and in this way represents the other things in succession, and teaches the readers by those words. In order that in that book one may observe closely this first of all, there are psalms that are said in narration, and those consisting of moral admonition, and those in prophecy, and those in prayer and those in confession. Those cast in the form of narrative are Psalms 18, 43, 48, 49, 72, 76, 88, 89, 106, 113, 126, and 136. Those in the form of prayer are 16, 67, 89, 101, 131, and 141. Those spoken in petition and in prayer and in entreaty are 5, 6, 7, 11, 12, 15, 24, 27, 30, 34, 37, 42, 53, 54, 55, 56, 58, 59, 60, 63, 82, 85, 87, 137, 139, and 142. And that in the mode of appeal and thanksgiving is 138. Those that feature petition only are 3, 25, 68, 69, 70, 73, 78, 79, 108, 122, 129, and 130. Psalms 9, 74, 91, 104, 105, 106, 107, 110, 117, 135, and 137 have the form of confession. Those having confession and narrative interwoven are 9, 74, 105, 106, 117, and 137. A psalm that has confession interwoven with narrative, along with praise, is 110. And Psalm 36 features exhortation. Those containing prophecy are 20, 21, 44, 46, and 75. In 109 there is announcement along with prophecy. The psalms that urge and prescribe are 28, 32, 80, 94, 95, 96, 97, 102, 103, and 113. Psalm 149 was spoken as exhortation combined with the singing of praise. Those expressing praise are 90, 112, 116, 134, 144, 145, 146, 148, and 150. Psalms 8, 9, 17, 33, 45, 62, 76, 84, 114, 115, 120, 121, 123, 125, 128, and 143 are songs of thanksgiving. Those announcing a promise of blessedness are 1, 31, 40, 118, and 127. Another demonstrative of holy readiness in song is Psalm 107. Psalm 80 is one that exhorts to courage. Those that lay charges against the impious and lawbreakers are 2, 13, 35, 51, and 52. And the fourth psalm has to do with invocation. There are also those that announce supplications to God, like 19 and 63. Those proclaiming words that boast in the Lord are 22, 26, 38, 39, 41, 61, 75, 83, 96, 98, and 151. Those that arouse a sense of shame are 57 and 81. And Psalms 47 and 64 voice the phrases of a hymn. Psalm 65 is one of exultation, and concerns resurrection. Another that speaks only exultant words is 99.

15. Therefore, since the arrangement of the Psalms is of such a kind, it is then possible for the readers (as I said before) to discover in each one the stirrings and the equanimity of the soul appropriate to them, just as they can discover in relation to each the type and teaching. And it can be learned, likewise, what one says to be able to gratify the Lord, and by what sort of expressions it is possible to make amends for himself and to return thanks to the Lord. All this is to prevent falling into impiety on the part of the one who speaks strictly according to such phrases. For not only because of deeds, but also because of idle speech, we are obliged to render an account to the Judge. And if you wish, moreover, to bless someone, you learn how you ought to do so, and in whose name, and what it is necessary to say, in Psalms 1, 31, 40, 111, 118, and 127. Should you wish to censure the treachery of the Jews against the Savior, you have the second psalm. If you are being persecuted by your own people, and you have many who rise up against you, say the third psalm. And if, being afflicted in this manner, you begged the Lord for help, and having been heeded, you desire to give thanks, sing the fourth, as well as Psalms 74 and 114. And whenever, spying the evildoers who want to set a trap for you, you want the Lord to hearken to your prayer, sing the fifth, rising early in the morning. And when you perceive a threatening from the Lord, should you see that you are disturbed for this reason, it is possible to say Psalms 6 and 37. And even if some people take counsel

against you, as Achitophel did against David, and someone reports this to you, sing Psalm 7 and place your confidence in the God who defends you.

16. When you behold the Savior's grace, which has been extended everywhere, and the human race, which has been rescued, if you wish to address the Lord, sing the eighth. And once more, if you wish to sing of the vintage, giving thanks to the Lord, you have the same Psalm 8, as well as the eighty-third. But in honor of conquest of the enemy and the preservation of creation, not boasting in yourself, but knowing the Son of God who accomplished this, recite the ninth psalm, which is spoken to him. Whenever someone seeks to provoke you excessively, hold your boldness in the Lord, and sing the tenth. And when you see the arrogance of the multitude and the evil that abounds, so that nothing is holy as far as men are concerned, flee to the Lord for refuge and say Psalm 11. But if the treachery that comes from your enemies becomes chronic, do not become neglectful, like one forgotten by God, but entreat the Lord, chanting the twelfth psalm. Should you hear people blaspheming against God's providence, do not share with them in their irreligion, but say Psalms 13 and 52, making your appeal to God. And then, if you wish to learn what sort of person the citizen of the kingdom of heaven is, chant Psalm 14.

17. Let us say you stand in need of a prayer because of those who have opposed you and encompass your soul; sing Psalms 16, 85, 87, and 140. Or you want to learn how Moses offered prayer—you have Psalm 89. You were preserved from your enemies, and you were delivered from your persecutors. Sing also Psalm 17. You marvel at the order of creation, and the grace of the providence in it, and the holy precepts of the Law. Sing the eighteenth and the twenty-third. When you see those who suffer tribulation,

encourage them, praying and speaking the words in Psalm 19. Should you become aware that you are being shepherded and led in the right path by the Lord, sing Psalm 22, rejoicing in this. Again, let us suppose the enemies are all around you. Nevertheless, lifting your soul up to God, say Psalm 24, and he sees that your adversaries commit their wrongs to no avail. They abide still, possessing nothing other than bloody hands, and seeking to wound and destroy you. Do not entrust to a man the judgment over them (for all things human are suspect), but counting God worthy to be judge (for he only is just), say the things in the twenty-fifth, thirty-fourth, and forty-second psalms. And if they savagely attack you, and the enemies become multitudinous, as rank upon rank, eyeing you with contempt, as if you have not yet been visited by grace—and on this account they wish to do battle—do not crouch in fear, but sing the twenty-sixth psalm. But since the nature of humankind is weak, should those who lay snares act shamelessly, call out to God in order that you may disregard them, reciting what is in Psalm 27. And if, in giving thanks, you wish to learn what it is necessary to offer to the Lord, while you think spiritually, chant the twenty-eighth. Further, when consecrating your house—that is, the soul that is being received by the Lord and the somatic house in which you dwell bodily—give thanks and say the twenty-ninth and the one hundred and twenty-sixth, which are among the gradual psalms.

18. When you see that you are despised and persecuted for the truth's sake by all your friends and relatives, do not give up concern either for them or for yourself. And if you see your acquaintances turning against you, do not be alarmed, but separate yourself from them and turn your mind to the future and sing Psalm 30. When you see those who are baptized and redeemed from their corrupt birth,

and you are filled with wonder over God's love for mankind, before these people sing your praise in the thirty-first psalm. If you wish to sing in the company of many, gathering men who are righteous and erect in their living, recite also Psalm 32. When you encounter your foes, and wisely escape them and avoid their treachery, if you want to express gratitude, summoning gentle men, sing Psalm 33 in their presence. Should you spy the zeal for evil among those who transgress the Law, do not think that the evil is in their very nature, which is what the heretics assert.[38] But say Psalm 36 and you will see that they themselves are responsible for the sinning. If you witness worthless people committing numerous lawless acts and exalting themselves against humbler people, and you wish to exhort someone not to devote himself to their service, nor to emulate them—for they are quickly vanished—say the thirty-sixth psalm both to yourself and to the others.

19. Then you also, when you propose to attend to yourself, if you should see the foe attacking (for at that time he is especially roused against such people), and should you wish to fortify yourself for the contest against him, recite Psalm 38. And if, when the enemies set upon you, you persevere in the face of the trials, and you want to learn the advantage of endurance, sing Psalm 39. But when you see numerous people in need and poverty, and you wish to treat them mercifully, you are able, by saying Psalm 40, both to approve those who already act with compassion, and to urge others toward doing the same. Possessing, then, a great desire for God, if you should hear the adversaries chiding you, do not be disturbed, but knowing the imperishable fruit that comes from such yearning, cheer on your own soul by the hope placed in God. And in that hope supporting and mollifying the soul's sorrows in life, say the forty-first psalm. Wishing unceasingly to re-

member the kind acts of God accomplished for the fathers, and, concerning the exodus from Egypt and the time passed in the wilderness, how God is good, but the men are ungrateful, you have Psalms 43, 77, 88, 104, 105, 106, and 113. And flying to God and being kept safe from the tribulations that take place around you, if you want to thank God and to recount the philanthropy that has come to you, you have the forty-fifth.

20. But you sinned, and being ashamed, you repent and you ask to be shown mercy. You have in Psalm 50 the words of confession and repentance. And even if you suffered calumny from a wicked ruler, and you see the slanderer boasting, withdraw from that place and say also the things in the fifty-first. When you are being pursued and certain ones are perpetrating slander, hoping to deliver you up to justice, as the Ziphites and the alien tribes did in the case of David,[39] do not succumb to weariness, but being confident in the Lord and hymning him, recite the things in Psalms 53 and 55. And even if your pursuer overtakes you, and without knowing it enters the cave in which you are hiding,[40] you should not even so cower in fear, for you have in such a necessity the memorially inscribed[41] words for encouragement found in Psalms 56 and 114. Should he who is plotting give the order for your house to be kept under surveillance, and you escape, express your gratitude to the Lord, inscribing it on your soul as on a monument—for it is a memorial to the fact that you were spared from destruction—and recite the verses in Psalm 58. And if the foes who afflict you hurl insults and the seeming friends, rising up, level accusations at you, and you are grieved in your meditation for a while,[42] nevertheless you also are able to be consoled, praising God and speaking the words of Psalm 54. Against those who posture and are outwardly boastful, say—for their humiliation—Psalm 57. But

against those rushing savagely toward you, desiring to seize your soul, render your obedience to God, and take courage. For the more they rage, the more you are to submit yourself to the Lord, and say what is in Psalm 61. And if, when persecuted, you go out into the desert, do not be afraid, as though alone, but having God there and rising before dawn, sing the sixty-second psalm.[43] When the enemies frighten you away, never ceasing from their lying in ambush, and also searching everywhere for you, even if they are vast in number, do not give way, for when you sing Psalms 63, 64, 69, and 70, *their wounds* will be caused by *the weapons of the foolish children.*[44]

21. Whenever you want to celebrate God in song, recite the things in Psalm 64. And if you wish to instruct some people about the resurrection, sing the words in Psalm 65. In chanting the sixty-sixth psalm, praise God while you beseech him to treat you mercifully. When you perceive the godless flourishing in peace and yet the righteous who suffer affliction living in complete dejection, say what is in the seventy-second psalm, lest you be caused to stumble and be shaken to the foundation. And whenever God's wrath is stirred against the people, you have for consolation in this circumstance the prudent words in Psalm 73. When you stand in need of confession of your sins, sing Psalms 9, 74, 91, 104, 105, 106, 107, 110, 117, 135, and 137. For the purpose of putting to shame the opinions of the Greeks and of the heretics, because the knowledge of God does not reside in a single one among them, but in the Catholic Church alone, you can, if you are so minded, sing and then recite the words in Psalm 75. But when the foes cut off your paths of escape, even if, being greatly oppressed, you are cast into confusion, do not despair, but pray. And when your cry is heard, thank God, reciting Psalm 76. Should the adversaries rush in and attack, and

continuing their aggression, pollute the house of God and slay the saints and hurl their bodies to the winged creatures of the heaven, in order that you not lie cowering, recoiled on yourself, before their cruelty, you must sympathize with those who suffer, and make your appeal to God, reciting the seventy-eighth psalm.

22. Wishing to praise the Lord in a festival, when you summon together the servants of God, sing the things in Psalms 80 and 94. And again, when the enemies are all gathered together from all points, and are both issuing threats against the house of God and forming a confederacy against true religion, lest you become despondent because of the magnitude of the crowd and its might, you possess as an anchor of hope the phrases in the eighty-second psalm. And seeing the house of God and his eternal tabernacles,[45] should you have zeal for these, as the Apostle did, say also the eighty-third psalm. After the wrath has abated and the captivity is ended, if you wish to give thanks, you have what is in Psalms 84 and 125 for the reciting. And if you want to know the excellence of the Church catholic in comparison with the convictions and actions of the schismatics, and to reprove the latter, you may say the words in the eighty-sixth. If you intend to make yourself bold and the others confident in right worship, since hope placed in God brings no shame, but instead makes the soul fearless, praise God with the expressions of Psalm 90. Do you wish to produce melody on the Sabbath? You have Psalm 91.

23. Do you wish to return thanks in the Lord's Day? You have the twenty-third. To chant your praises on the second day of the week? Recite Psalm 47.[46] Do you seek to glorify God in the day of preparation? You have the praise written in Psalm 92. For at that time when the crucifixion occurred, the house of God was built up, indeed, to hold

120

off the enemies that assault it. On account of this victory it is fitting to sing to God, using the things said then in Psalm 92, and when captivity befalls you, should the house be destroyed and built once again, chant what is in Psalm 95.[47] When the land is secured by the warriors and thereafter remains tranquil, and the Lord reigns—if you wish to offer your praises for this, you have Psalm 96. Do you want to sing on the fourth day of the week? You have the ninety-third. For at that time the Lord began to exact vengeance, handing down the punishment unto death, and to declare himself in bold speech. When, therefore, while reading the Gospel, you see the Jews taking counsel in the fourth day of the week against the Lord, as you perceive him then speaking openly in punishment of the devil for our sake, chant the things bearing on this in Psalm 93. Seeing, again, the Lord's providence and his rulership in all things, and wishing to educate some people for trust and obedience in him, and prevailing upon them first to confess their faith, sing Psalm 99. And after coming to know his power for judging, and that the Lord makes a decision, tempering the judgment with mercy, should you wish to approach him, you have the words of Psalm 100 for this purpose.

24. Since our nature is feeble, when you come to be like a beggar because of life's distresses, if at some time you are exhausted and you wish to be encouraged, you have the one hundred and first psalm. And since it is appropriate for us to give thanks to God through and in all circumstances, when you wish to commend him, for this you must urge your own soul forward, and say Psalms 102 and 103. Do you want to give voice to your praise, and to know how and to whom it is necessary to express it, and what things it is fitting to say in the commendation? You have Psalms 104, 106, 134, 145, 146, 147, 148, and 150. Have you faith, as the Lord said, and when praying do you believe those

121

things you are speaking? Say the one hundred and fifteenth. Do you perceive yourself as one who is progressing by deeds, so as to say, I forget *what lies behind and* I strain forward *to what lies ahead?*[48] For each advance you may recite the fifteen odes among the gradual psalms.

25. You were enthralled by foreign thoughts, and you perceived yourself as one being seduced, and in repentance determining to desist from this in the future (though remaining among those who seized you when you were in error) now you must sit still and utter your lament, as the people of Israel did then, reciting what is in Psalm 136. When you think of temptations as a testing for you, if you want to give thanks after the trials, you have the one hundred and thirty-eighth psalm. You might find yourself beleaguered once more by the enemies. Do you want to be rescued? Recite Psalm 139. Do you want to offer up supplications and prayers? Chant Psalms 5 and 142. Should a tyrannical foe rise up against the people and against you, as Goliath against David, do not tremble in fear. You too must have faith, like David, and say the things in Psalm 143. After marveling at the kindnesses of God in all things and recalling his benevolence, which affects you and all the rest, if you wish to commend God on account of these, say David's words that he spoke himself in the one hundred and forty-fourth psalm. You want to address your praises to the Lord? For your recitation you have Psalms 92 and 97. If, though insignificant, you are selected for some sovereignty over your brothers, do not be exalted against them, but attributing the glory to God who chose you, chant Psalm 151, which is David's own. Let us say you want to sing those psalms that contain the alleluia to indicate how God has answered prayer[49]—you may employ Psalms 104, 105, 106, 111, 112, 113, 114, 115, 117, 118, 134, 135, 145, 146, 147, 148, 149, and 150.

26. When you desire, in private, to extol the events concerning the Savior, you find such things in nearly every psalm, but you have particularly Psalms 44 and 109, which show forth his true generation from the Father and his incarnate appearance. There are Psalms 21 and 68, which foretell about the divine cross and what great treachery he submitted to on our behalf, and the number of things he suffered; and Psalms 2 and 108, which signal both the plotting and wickedness of the Jews and the betrayal by Judas Iscariot; and the twentieth, forty-ninth, and seventy-first, also making manifest his kingship, his power as judge and, again, his appearance in flesh for us, and also the calling of the gentiles. Psalm 15 demonstrates his resurrection from the dead. The twenty-third and forty-sixth announce his ascent into heaven, and while reading Psalms 92, 95, 97, and 98 you should be able to contemplate the benefits won for us by the Savior through his sufferings.

27. Such, then, is the character of the assistance for mankind to be gained from the Book of Psalms, which contains psalms peculiar to itself, and has in the remainder more frequent prophecies concerning the bodily advent of our Lord and Savior, Jesus Christ, as I said earlier. It is important not to pass over the question of why words of this kind are chanted with melodies and strains. For some of the simple among us, although they believe indeed that the phrases are divinely inspired, imagine, however, on account of the sweetness of sound, that also the psalms are rendered musically for the sake of the ear's delight. But this is not so. For Scripture did not seek out that which is pleasant and winning, but this also has been fashioned for the benefit of the soul, and for all number of reasons, but especially on account of two. First, because it is fitting for the Divine Scripture to praise God not in compressed speech alone, but also in the voice that is richly broadened.

Things are said, then, in close sequence; such are all the contents of the Law and the Prophets and the histories, along with the New Testament. On the other hand, things are expressed more broadly; of this kind are the phrases of the psalms, odes, and songs. For thus will it be preserved that men love God with their whole strength and power. The second reason is that, just as harmony that unites flutes effects a single sound, so also, seeing that different movements appear in the soul—and in it is the power of reasoning, and eager appetite, and high-spirited passion,[50] from the motion of which comes also the activity of the parts of the body—the reason intends man neither to be discordant in himself, nor to be at variance with himself. So the most excellent things derive from reasoning, while the most worthless derive from acting on the basis of desire, as is the case with Pilate when he says, *I find no crime in him*,[51] and yet concurs in the purpose of the Jews. A person either craves the commonest things but is unable to do them, like the elders in the story of Susanna; or again he does not commit adultery, but he steals; or he forgoes stealing in favor of committing murder, or he does no murder, but commits blasphemy.

28. In order that some such confusion not occur in us, the reason intends the soul that possesses the mind of Christ, as the Apostle said,[52] to use this as a leader, and by it both to be a master of its passions and to govern the body's members, so as to comply with reason. Thus, as in music there is a plectrum, so the man becoming himself a stringed instrument and devoting himself completely to the Spirit may obey in all his members and emotions, and serve the will of God. The harmonious reading of the Psalms is a figure and type of such undisturbed and calm equanimity of our thoughts. For just as we discover the ideas of the soul and communicate them through the words

we put forth, so also the Lord, wishing the melody of the words to be a symbol of the spiritual harmony in a soul, has ordered that the odes be chanted tunefully, and the Psalms recited with song. The desire of the soul is this—to be beautifully disposed, as it is written: *Is anyone among you cheerful? Let him sing praise.*[53] In this way that which is disturbing and rough and disorderly in it is smoothed away, and that which causes grief is healed when we sing psalms. *Why are you very sad, O my soul, and why do you trouble me?*[54] That which causes stumbling will be discovered, as it says, *But my feet were almost overthrown.*[55] With regard to what he fears, he gains strength from hope by saying, *The Lord is my helper, and I will not fear what man shall do to me.*[56]

29. Those who do not recite the divine songs in this manner do not sing them wisely. They bring delight to themselves, but they incur blame, because *a hymn of praise is not suitable on the lips of a sinner.*[57] But when they chant in the way mentioned earlier, so that the melody of the phrases is brought forth from the soul's good order and from the concord with the Spirit, such people sing with the tongue, but singing also with the mind they greatly benefit not only themselves but even those willing to hear them. Blessed David, then, making music in this way for Saul, was himself well pleasing to God, and he drove away from Saul the troubled and frenzied disposition, making his soul calm. The priests who sang thus summoned the souls of the people into tranquillity, and called them into unanimity with those who form the heavenly chorus. Therefore the Psalms are not recited with melodies because of a desire for pleasant sounds. Rather, this is a sure sign of the harmony of the soul's reflections. Indeed, the melodic reading is a symbol of the mind's well-ordered and undisturbed condition. Moreover, the praising of God in well-tuned cymbals and harp and ten-stringed instrument was again a

figure and sign of the parts of the body coming into natural concord like harp strings, and of the thoughts of the soul becoming like cymbals, and then all of these being moved and living through the grand sound and through the command of the Spirit so that, as it is written, the man lives in the Spirit and mortifies the deeds of the body.[58] For thus beautifully singing praises, he brings rhythm to his soul and leads it, so to speak, from disproportion to proportion, with the result that, due to its steadfast nature, it is not frightened by something, but rather imagines positive things, even possessing a full desire for the future goods. And gaining its composure by the singing of the phrases, it becomes forgetful of the passions and, while rejoicing, sees in accordance with the mind of Christ, conceiving the most excellent thoughts.

30. Now, my son, it is necessary for each of the readers of that book to read it in its entirety, for truly the things in it are divinely inspired, but then to take benefits from these, as from the fruits of a garden on which he may cast his gaze when the need arises. For I believe that the whole of human existence, both the dispositions of the soul and the movements of the thoughts, have been measured out and encompassed in those very words of the Psalter. And nothing beyond these is found among men. For whether there was necessity of repentance or confession, or tribulation and trial befell us, or someone was persecuted, or, being plotted against, he was protected, or if, moreover, someone has become deeply sorrowful and disturbed and he suffers something of the sort that is described in the things just mentioned, and he either attends to himself as one who is advancing, being set free from his foe, or he wants to sing praises and give thanks to the Lord—for any such eventuality he has instruction in the divine Psalms. Let him therefore select the things said in them about each

of these circumstances, and reciting what has been written as concerning him, and being affected by the writings, lift them up to the Lord.

31. Do not let anyone amplify these words of the Psalter with the persuasive phrases of the profane, and do not let him attempt to recast or completely change the words. Rather let him recite and chant, without artifice, the things written just as they were spoken, in order for the holy men who supplied these, recognizing that which is their own, to join you in your prayer, or, rather, so that even the Spirit who speaks in the saints, seeing words inspired by him in them, might render assistance to us. For as much better as the life of the saints is than that of other people, by so much also are their expressions superior to those we construct and, if one were to speak the truth, more powerful as well. For they greatly pleased God in these, and when saying them, as the Apostle put it, *they conquered kingdoms, enforced justice, received promises, stopped the mouths of lions, quenched raging fire, escaped the edge of the sword, won strength out of weakness, became mighty in war, put foreign armies to flight, and women received their dead by resurrection.*[59]

32. Therefore, reciting even now the same words, let each person be confident, for God will pay heed quickly to those who make supplications through these. Whether one is afflicted at the time he recites these things, he will regard as great the encouragement that is in them; or whether he is tested and persecuted while chanting thus, he will be shown forth as more worthy, and will be protected by the Lord, who watched over the one who originally said these things. In these he will overthrow the devil, and he will drive away his demons. By saying these things if he sinned, he will reprove himself and stop; but if he did not sin, he will see himself as one rejoicing. And he strains forward to *what lies ahead,*[60] and contending for the prize he will be

strengthened when he sings in that way, and will not be shaken from the truth forever, but he will even bring to disgrace those who deceive and those who seize you, hoping to lead you into error. And of this man is not a guarantor, but the Divine Scripture itself. For God commanded Moses to write the great song[61] and to teach it to the people, and he orders the one who is established as ruler to write Deuteronomy, to hold this in his hands, and to diligently obey its contents forever,[62] since the words in it are sufficient both for recalling virtue to the mind and for bringing help to those who sincerely heed them. For instance, at the time Joshua entered the land, he saw the battle array of the enemy and all the rulers of the Amorites amassed for war.[63] And confronted by the camps and swords he read Deuteronomy into all ears, calling the words of the Law to remembrance, and arming the people with them, and he prevailed over the foes. And King Josiah, when the book was discovered and was read in the hearing of all, was no longer afraid of the enemy.[64] And if at some time there was war in the land, the ark containing the tablets of Law went before them all, and provided sufficient help to them in the face of every army, unless someone was alongside its bearers, and sin and hypocrisy, which were prevalent beforehand, were in the people.[65] For theirs must be a disposition of faith and genuineness so that the Law may work in favor of the things sought through prayer.

33. The old man said, "Indeed, I have heard from wise men how long ago in Israel they drove demons away and turned aside the treacheries directed against them by merely reading the Scriptures." For this reason he said those deserve judgment who abandon them, fashioning phrases meant to be persuasive in the pagan style, and naming themselves exorcists in the use of these. They indulge

themselves too much in play, and they expose themselves to being mocked by those demons. How the Jews, the sons of Sceva, suffered when they attempted to exorcise in this manner![66] When hearing these things issuing from such men, the demons began their sport with them, but they feared the words of the saints, and were not even able to endure them. For the Lord is in the phrases of the Scriptures, and since they cannot withstand him, they cry out, *I beseech you, do not torment me before the time.*[67] For seeing the Lord present, they were consumed. So Paul commanded the unclean spirits,[68] and likewise things demonic were subjected to the disciples.[69] And the hand of the Lord came over Elisha the prophet, and he prophesied about the waters to the three kings,[70] when he who chanted was singing in accordance with the Lord's command. So also now, if someone is concerned for those who suffer, and he recites these things himself, he also will benefit the sufferer more, and will show his faith to be true and steadfast, with the result that God, seeing that, supplies perfect healing to those in need. Knowing this, the holy one said in the one hundred and eighteenth psalm: *I will meditate on your ordinances; I will not forget your words.*[71] And again, *Your ordinances were my songs in the place of my sojourning.*[72] For in those they were gaining salvation, saying, *Were it not that your law is my meditation, then I should have perished in my affliction.*[73] It was for this reason also that Paul fortified his own disciple by these things, saying, *Practice these duties, devote yourself to them, so that your progress may become manifest.*[74] You too, practicing these things and reciting the Psalms intelligently in this way, are able to comprehend the meaning in each, being guided by the Spirit. And the kind of life the holy, God-bearing men possessed who spoke these things—this life you also shall imitate.

Notes

INTRODUCTION

1. See the account of the issues raised, particularly by a study in 1877 by H. Weingarten, in K. Heussi, *Der Ursprung des Mönchtums* (Tübingen, 1936), chap. 3. Among other things, it has long puzzled students that Athanasius mentions Antony only one other time in his extensive writings—and that in a passage that parallels chap. 87 of the *Vita Antonii* (see text, and note 146).

2. The career of Athanasius is sketched in F. L. Cross, *The Study of Athanasius* (Oxford, 1945) and H. von Campenhausen, *The Fathers of the Greek Church*, trans. S. Godman (New York, 1955), pp. 67–79. A helpful survey of the complicated turns taken in fortunes of the parties embroiled in the Arian controversy is found in H. Chadwick, *The Early Church* (Baltimore, Md.: 1967), chaps. 8–9.

3. The usual dating of 357 is endorsed in J. Quasten, *Patrology* (Antwerp, 1966), vol. 3, p. 39. A time of composition between 365 and 373 was proposed by A. von Hertling in *Antonius der Einseidler* (Innsbruck, 1929). (The debate continues in articles by L. W. Barnard and B. R. Brennan in volumes 28 and 30 of *Vigiliae Christianae*.) See the opening section of *Life of Antony* (*Vita Antonii*, or VA) for Athanasius's description of the request to which he is responding.

4. For his provocative treatment of the early Egyptian monastic phenomenon as a "crisis in human relations" in which the desire for disengagement mirrored typical village attitudes, see P. Brown, *The Making of Late Antiquity* (Cambridge, Mass., 1978), pp. 81–101.

5. Owen Chadwick, *John Caissian*, 2nd ed. (Cambridge, 1967), p. 3.

6. See Brown, *Making of Late Antiquity*, pp. 89–98. Also, A. C. Baynes, "St. Antony and the Demons," *Journal of Egyptian Archaeology* 40 (1954): 7ff.

131

NOTES

7. These are the views expressed in treatments by L. Bouyer, *La Spiritualité du Nouveau Testament et des Péres*, Historie de la Spiritualité Chrétienne 1 (Aubier, 1966), chap. 13, and by B. Steidle, "Homo Dei Antonius," in *Antonius Magnus Eremita, 356–1956*, Studia Anselmiana 38 (Rome, 1956), pp. 182–183.

8. Bouyer, *Spiritualité*, p. 368

9. So, respectively, were the contentions of: R. Reitzenstein, *Des Athanasius Werk über das Leben des Antonius* (Heidelberg, 1914); K. Holl, *Die schriftstellerische Form des griechischen Heiligenlebens* (Tübingen, 1928); J. List, *Das Antoniusleben des hl. Athanasius des Grossen* (Athens, 1931); S. Cavallin, *Literarhistorische und textkritische Studien zur Vita Caesarii Arelatensis* (Lund, 1934).

10. Quasten, *Patrology*, vol. 3, p. 43, writes: "It would be difficult to trace the literary influence in detail, although there cannot be any doubt that the classical model of the hero's *Vita* as well as the newer type of *Vita* of the sage served as an inspiration for Athanasius. But it remains his great achievement that he recasted these inherited expressions of popular ideals in the Christian mold and disclosed the same heroism in the imitator of Christ aided by the power of grace. Thus he created a new type of biography that was to serve as a model for all subsequent Greek and Latin hagiography."

11. So runs the argument of List, *Antoniusleben.*

12. See VA chap. 69, and note 128.

13. Hermann Dörries, *Die Vita Antonii als Geschichtsquelle*, Nachrichten der Akademie der Wissenschaften in Göttingen 14 (Göttingen, 1949), p. 389.

14. Brown, *Making of Late Antiquity*, p. 90.

15. See P. Brown, "The Rise and Function of the Holy Man in Late Antiquity," *Journal of Roman Studies* 61 (1971): 80–101 and especially p. 91.

16. Ibid., p. 91.

17. This consideration of the fruit of one's labor was not peculiar to Christian ascetic theory alone, as is pointed out in A. Meredith, "Asceticism—Christian and Greek," *Journal of Theological Studies*, new series 27.2 (1976), 320: "The final point that needs making about ascesis is the result that accrues to the ascetic in terms of increased spiritual power. In the case of Antony this power meant two things: the power to deal with demons by discerning them and then expelling them, and secondly miraculous powers over various forms of illness. In chapter

NOTES

84 of the *Vita* we read of the miracles he worked and the discernment he displayed. The author, however, is careful to remark at the outset that 'it was clear to all that it was not he himself who worked, but the Lord who showed mercy by his means and healed the sufferer' (cf. also chap. 38). Antony's part was only prayer and discipline. Even with this qualification such a claim is not very far from that advanced for the ascetic by Porphyry in *De Abs.* ii.49. The true philosopher, he writes, is a priest of the supreme God, and by his abstinence he is united to the God he serves. This union gives him great powers of judgment and knowledge of the secret things of nature. More explicitly, he writes in *Ad Marcellam* 11 that 'to the wise man God gives power.' The only difference between the sage and the saint is less one of practice than of theory. The saint becomes God's instrument (V.A. 83): the sage becomes his agent—descriptively they are barely distinct." There is an important factor in Athanasius's "qualification," however, that is more intelligible in the light of the sharp differences that separated orthodox and early Arian Christians.

18. See note 128 for the text of VA, and the remarks of Dörries, *Vita Antonius als Geschichtsquelle,* p. 390.

19. For a more extensive treatment, see R. Gregg and D. Groh, *Early Arianism—A View of Salvation* (Philadelphia, 1980), chap 4.

20. See VA, chap. 69.

21. Bishop Alexander of Alexandria (Athanasius's predecessor) denies that Christ is Son in the same way that believers can claim to be sons. He writes *(Ep. ad. Alex):* ". . . his sonship, which is endowed with the paternal divinity by nature *(kata phusin)* surpasses by an inexpressible preeminence the sonship of those who have been adopted as sons through his appointment *(di autou thesei)*. He is, on the one hand, unchangeable, being perfect and sufficient in all respects, while they, on the other hand, liable to [the] turning in both directions, stand in need of his assistance *(boētheia)*."

22. In his *Orations against the Arians* 3.51, Athanasius asserts that anyone able to partake of the divine brilliance of God's son "one ray, so to speak . . . becomes all-perfect among men, and equal to angels."

23. See VA, chap. 7, and note 24.

24. See Gregory Naz. *Or.* 21.5; Palladius *Hist. Laus.* 8; *Vita Pachom.* 99, trans. A. A. Athanassakis, *The Life of Pachomius,* Society of Biblical Literature Texts and Translations 7, Early Christian Literature Series 2 (Missoula, Mont., 1975), p. 41.

25. Jerome *De vir. ill.* 87, 88, 125.

26. See the remarks of O. Chadwick, *John Cassian*, p. 4. The text attributed to Evagrius is printed beneath the Greek text in Migne's *Patrologia Graeca* 26, cols. 835–976. The other Latin version appears in G. Garitte, *Un témoin important du texte de la Vie de S. Antoine*, Études de philologie, d'archéologie et d'histoire anciennes 3 (Brussels, 1939).

27. Augustine *Conf.* 8.6, trans. R. S. Pine-Coffin, *Saint Augustine, Confessions* (Baltimore, Maryland, 1961), p. 168.

28. J. Leclercq, *The Love of Learning and the Desire for God*, trans. C. Misrahi, 2nd rev. ed. (New York, 1974), p. 125.

29. G. Ferrari, "Sources for the Early Iconography of St. Antony," in *Antonius Magnus Eremita, 395–1956*, ed. B. Steidle, Studia Anselmiana 38 (Rome, 1956): 248–253.

30. See W. Braunfels, *Lexikon der Christlichen Ikonographie 5*, Ikonographie der Heiligen (Rome, 1973), cols. 205–217. Also L. Réau, *Iconographie de l'Art Chrétien* 3, Iconographie des Saints (Paris, 1958), pp. 100–115. Réau suggests (pp. 109–110) that the opportunity to treat erotic subjects was a factor in artists' enthusiasm for this theme, as well as for the stories of Susanna and the daughters of Lot.

31. See Athanasius *Apologia c. Arianos* 73, which lists a Marcellinus among the deacons of Alexandria. The name, however, was common.

32. Athanasius *Orationes c. Arianos* 1.11.

33. See the use of lines from the Psalter, for example, in festal letters, 3, 7, 11, 14; in A. Robertson, ed., *Select Writings and Letters of Athanasius, Bishop of Alexandria*, A Select Library of Nicene and Post-Nicene Fathers of the Christian Church, Second Series 4 (New York, 1892; rev. ed. Grand Rapids, Mich., 1957), pp. 512ff.

34. See R. P. C. Hanson, "Biblical Exegesis in the Early Church," in *The Cambridge History of the Bible*, vol. 1, ed. P. R. Ackroyd and C. F. Evans (Cambridge: 1970), pp. 419–422.

ATHANASIUS' LIFE OF ANTONY

1. The title was selected from several headings of Greek manuscripts by the editors of the Migne text. See PG 26, 835.

2. Peter Brown has sketched vividly the factors involved in the rise to prominence of monks in the Later Empire, arguing that such

NOTES

figures as Antony and Symeon Stylites in Syria performed functions of the "good patron," the *prostatēs*, in Late Roman rural situations. Signs of Antony's role as arbiter and mediator appear at various points in the VA, but most graphically in chapter 84, in which he is called on by judges. See P. Brown, "The Rise and Function of the Holy Man in Late Antiquity," *Journal of Roman Studies* 61 (1971): 80–101.

3. In 4 Kings 3:11 (EB 2 Kings 3:11), Elisha is referred to as one who "poured water on the hands of Elijah." It is difficult to know what this statement conveys about the author's relationship to his subject, or to draw firm conclusions about the frequency and duration of his meetings with the monk. It is striking that only once in the treatise does Athanasius suggest that he was a witness to the events described (see note 132).

4. Cf. Gen. 25:27.

5. Mt. 4:20; Acts 4:35; Mt. 19:21.

6. Mt. 19:21.

7. In general terms, *aroura* signifies arable land, but here the reference is to an Egyptian measure of land, i.e., 100 square cubits. R. T. Meyer, in *St. Athanasius, The Life of Saint Antony* (ACW, 10), p. 107, calculates that the property of Antony's family was the equivalent of 207 acres.

8. Cf. Gal. 4:18.

9. 2 Thess. 3:10.

10. Combining ideas in 1 Thess. 5:17 and Mt. 6:7.

11. Job 40:11 (LXX).

12. See chap. 20, and Athanasius *C. Gent.* 30–31.

13. 1 Cor. 15:10.

14. In addition to continuing prevailing Greco-Roman attitudes about blacks and about the Ethiopians, Christian writers (like the Jewish community at Qumran) elaborated the imagery of spiritual darkness and light in numerous ways. See F. M. Snowden, *Blacks in Antiquity: Ethiopians in the Greco-Roman Experience* (Cambridge, Mass.: 1970), esp. chap. 9. Is there implicit in this episode the suggestion that the black youth represents the practice of pederasty?

15. Hos. 4:12.

16. Ps. 117:7.

17. Rom. 8:3–4.

18. Cf. 1 Cor. 9:27.

19. 2 Cor. 12:10.

NOTES

20. Phil. 3:13. For the importance of this Pauline Text in Alexandrian and Cappadocian Christian writings, see R. E. Heine, *Perfection in the Virtuous Life*, Patristic Monograph Series 2 (Cambridge, Mass.: 1975), esp. pp. 241ff.

21. A combination of language found in 3 Kings 17:1 and 18:15 of the Septuagint (EB: 1 Kings).

22. Cf. Rom. 8:35.

23. Ps. 26:3.

24. This saving ray or beam *(aktina phōtos)* appears elsewhere in Athanasian writings (notably *Or. c. Ar.* 3.51) as part of a criticism of Arian Christology. For an analysis of anti-Arian interests in the *Life of Antony*, see R. Gregg and D. Groh, *Early Arianism—A View of Salvation* (Philadelphia, 1980), chapter 4: "Claims on the Life of St. Antony."

25. Ps. 67:1–2.

26. Ps. 117:10.

27. From Libanius's works Peter Brown draws examples of the patron's use of his power "to smooth over the thorny issues of village life. He would provide—and help distribute—the all important water supply of the village. He would arrange the cancelling of debts. He could settle disputes among the villagers on the spot, and so save them the long trek to the local town to conduct their litigation" (Brown, "The Rise and Function of the Holy Man in Late Antiquity," p. 85).

28. Rom. 8:32.

29. Arsinoë and its canal, which connected Lake Moeris and the Nile, stood in Arcadia to the west of the River some 150 miles south of Alexandria, and was also known as Crocodilopolis!

30. Ps. 89:10.

31. Cf. 1 Cor. 15:42.

32. Rom. 8:18.

33. Eccles. 4:8, 6:2.

34. Luke 17:7ff.

35. Ezek. 3:20, 33:12ff., 18:26.

36. Cf. Rom. 8:28.

37. 1 Cor. 15:31.

38. Cf. Phil. 3:13.

39. Lk. 9:62.

40. Lk. 17:21.

41. Josh. 24:23.

NOTES

42. Mt. 3:3.
43. Jas. 1:20, 1:15.
44. Prov. 3:23.
45. Eph. 6:16.
46. See 1 Cor. 12:7, 10.
47. 2 Cor. 2:11.
48. Job 41:9–12.
49. Job 41:22–23.
50. Ex. 15:9.
51. Is. 10:14.
52. Cf. Job 40:20.
53. Cf. Job 40:24.
54. Hab. 2:15.
55. Lk. 4:41.
56. Cf. Jude 6.
57. Ps. 49:16.
58. Ps. 38:1–2.
59. Ps. 38:14.
60. Cf. Jn. 8:44.
61. Ecclus. 1:24.
62. 4 Kings 19:35 (EB: 2 Kings 19:35).
63. Job 2:7. See Job 1–2.
64. Mk. 5:12.
65. Lk. 10:19 (nearly exact).
66. In the Septuagint, History of Susanna 42 (EB: Apocrypha—Susanna 42).
67. 2 Kings 18:24ff. (EB: 2 Sam. 18:24ff.).
68. Athanasius is able to draw on earlier Christian considerations of reliable and unreliable predictions and prophecies, for example, Origen *C. Cels.* 4.92ff. and 7.2ff. See also Athanasius's remarks in *De Inc.* 46–47, 55.
69. 4 Kings 5:26 (EB: 2 Kings 5:26).
70. 4 Kings 6:17 (EB: 2 Kings 6:17).
71. Cf. Col. 2:15.
72. On *daemones* in late antiquity and early Christian writing, see E. R. Dodds, *Pagan and Christian in an Age of Anxiety,* chaps. 2 and 3 (Cambridge, 1965), and J. Danielou, *Origen,* Part 3, chaps. 1–3 (New York, 1955).

73. Mt. 12:19; cf. Is. 42:2.

74. Cf. 1 Cor. 1:24 and see chap. 40 in this document, where the tall demon presents himself to Antony as God's "power."

75. See Lk. 1:13.

76. See Mk. 16:6.

77. See Lk. 2:10.

78. "Dejection" is the inadequate translation for *akēdia* (or, later, "accidie"), which Cassian treats extensively in Book 10 of *Institutes*. This torpor of the spirit is noted as a problem in Palladius's *Lausiac History*, in the prologue and in chapters 5, 16, and 21 (in which Cronius, a priest of Nitria, tells how he visited Antony's mountain when he fled his monastery because of *akēdia*).

79. Cf. Mt. 4:9.

80. Mt. 4:10.

81. Lk. 10:20.

82. Mt. 7:22.

83. See Mt. 7:22.

84. Cf. Ps. 1:6.

85. 1 Jn. 4:1.

86. Antony must certify his feats and yet evade the charge of pride and vainglory. The model for his presentation is 2 Cor. 10–12.

87. Ps. 19:7.

88. Ps. 37:13.

89. Cf. Rom. 8:35.

90. Lk. 10:18.

91. 1 Cor. 4:6.

92. Ps. 9:6.

93. Josh. 5:13.

94. Susanna 51–59 (LXX).

95. The connection between withdrawal (*anachōrēsis*) into the desert and absence of tax collectors is quite direct in Coptic Egypt. "The word which the tax-gatherers used . . . in telling of the desertion of the tax-subjects in their villages has an interesting history. It is *anachoresan*, literally, 'they have gone up,' that is, up from the river valley into the desert. It may be worth our while to note the changing meaning of this word. Always it refers to a physical withdrawal, a retreat. In the Ptolemaic period this 'going away' was a group action, carried out as a challenge to irritating and oppressive conditions imposed by the government. Almost always, so far as our knowledge goes, this group-protest,

NOTES

with threats of work cessation, was successful. In the Roman period the 'going up,' or flight, was purely individual, an individual withdrawal from official oppression, that is, an individual's means of escape from the lay yoke of physical and financial burdens. In the Byzantine-Coptic literature of Christianized Egypt the word 'anchorite' is its derivative. The 'anchorite' is the man who has 'gone up,' retreated into caves or dens of the desert's edge. The suggestion that he was merely emulating the forty days of solitude in the desert of Jesus of Nazareth or the ascetic life of John the Baptist is not adequate" (W. L. Westermann, "On the Background of Coptism," in *Coptic Egypt* [Brooklyn, N.Y., 1941], pp. 12–13).

96. Num. 24:5–6.

97. Lk. 12:22, 29–31.

98. Exercising his rule in the East of the Empire, Maximin was Caesar from 305–308, Augustus from 308–313. Eusebius of Caesarea writes of the persecution in *De martyribus Palaestinae*. A. H. M. Jones says of Maximin: "[he] was a determined pagan and soon renewed the attack [after Galerius' death in 311] in a more constructive way. He gave paganism the organization which it had hitherto lacked by appointing an official high priest for each city and a superior high priest for each province. He published spurious Acts of Pilate and ordered them to be taught in the schools. He obtained and publicized confessions from prostitutes that they had participated in Christian orgies. He graciously acceded to petitions from Nicomedia, Tyre and other large cities and even from entire provinces that Christians should be expelled from their boundaries. After these preliminaries the persecution began again in earnest. Maximin was opposed to executions and preferred to condemn recusants to the mines and quarries after blinding one eye and ham-stringing one leg, but there were a few martyrdoms. This persecution was revoked by Maximin after his defeat by Licinius in 313, shortly before his death" (A. H. M. Jones, *The Decline of the Ancient World* [London, 1966], p. 37. See Eusebius *De martyr. Palaest.*, and W. H. C. Frend, *Martyrdom and Persecution in the Early Church* [New York, 1967], pp. 377–392).

99. From an early point there was suspicion within the Church of those who were too eager for martyrdom. Antony's unwillingness "to hand himself over" is more dramatically presented in the nearly ritual attempts of Bishop Polycarp to evade his pursuers in *Mart. Polycarp* 5–6. The author of the martyrology states clearly in the preceding

NOTES

section: "Therefore brethren, we do not commend those who surrender themselves, for such is not the teaching of the Gospel." The Council of Elvira in Spain in 305 reached the decision that overzealous Christians whose provocative actions involved the smashing of idols were not to be regarded, if apprehended and punished, as martyrs. For a description of the devotion to martyrdom among the "circumcellions" in the Donatist Church of North Africa, see W. H. C. Frend, *The Donatist Church* (Oxford, 1971), pp. 172ff. Cf. P. Brown, "Religious Dissent in the Later Roman Empire: The Case of North Africa," and "Religious Coercion in the Later Roman Empire: The Case of North Africa," in *Religion and Society in the Age of Saint Augustine* (New York, 1972) pp. 237–259 and 301–331.

100. Two terms in the last phrase hold particular interest: *propempein* frequently is used in reference to a funeral procession in which one follows a corpse to the grave, and *teleiōthōsin* (from *teleisō*) connotes completion, fulfillment and perfection—and therefore death. The latter word is employed in early Christian literature (e.g., Heb. 12:23) to describe a good death—that is, a fitting end to a faithful life (which has its rewards).

101. Peter was bishop of Alexandria from 300 or 301 until he was beheaded in 311 and (as Eusebius writes in *H.E.* 7.32.31) was "so adorned with the crown of martyrdom." Peter's withdrawal from the city during persecution made it possible for Meletius, bishop of Lycopolis, to assume the responsibilities of his office, resulting in the dispute that is associated with Meletius's name (see note 127).

102. Lk. 11:9.

103. Antony's intention, according to Athanasius, is to move to the south, in the direction of ancient Thebes on the Nile.

104. "The Pastures," or *ta boukolia*, refers to a marshy district in the Nile Delta. See K. Sethe, *"Boukoloi,"* *Realenzyklopädie der classischen Altertumswissenschaft*, vol. 3 (1898): 1013.

105. Described in Jerome *Vita S. Hilar.*, 30 ff., Antony's "inner mountain" is identified as Mt. Colzim, which retains the name Dêr Mar Antonios and is positioned between the Nile and the Red Sea some 160 miles from the Mediterranean coast. (See map.)

106. Eph. 6:12.

107. Ps. 124:1.

108. See Job 5:23.

109. Prov. 24:15b.

NOTES

110. Eph. 4:26.
111. See 2 Cor. 13:5.
112. 1 Cor. 4:5 and Rom. 2:16.
113. Gal. 6:2.
114. Cf. 1 Cor. 9:27.
115. See Mt. 9:20.
116. The historian Sozomen tells us *(H.E.* 1.10.) that Paphnutius, the ascetic bishop of the Upper Thebaid, had been brutalized during the persecution by Maximin, losing his right eye and use of his left leg. His status as confessor no doubt enhanced his authority at Nicaea in 325, where (we are told) he rose to speak against a canon calling for clergy to "put away" their wives: "He said that marriage was honorable and chaste, and that cohabitation with their own wives was chastity, and advised the Synod not to frame such a law, for it would be difficult to bear, and might serve as an occasion for incontinence to them and their wives; and he reminded them, that according to the ancient tradition of the church, those who were unmarried when they took part in the communion of sacred orders, were required to remain so, but that those who were married, were not to put away their wives" (Sozomen *H.E.* 1.23, NPNF translation). For an interesting glimpse of the impact of asceticism (and its lore) on the imagination of a fifth-century Christian historian, see also Book 3.14 in the same work.
117. Amun was one of the prominent ascetics from the desert of Nitria. The story of his wedding night and the compact of virginity made with his bride is told in Palladius, *Lausiac History* 8 and in Socrates *H.E.* 4.23. On the strength of Amun's appeal, according to Socrates, the mountains of Nitria and Scete became a center of monastic activity.
118. Eph. 2:2.
119. Eph. 6:13; Tit. 2:8.
120. 2 Cor. 12:3.
121. 2 Cor. 12:4.
122. Jn. 6:45.
123. Phil. 3:13.
124. Prov. 15:13.
125. Gen. 31:5.
126. See 1 Kings 16:12 (EB: 1 Sam. 16:12).
127. The Meletian (frequently called Melitian) schism grew out of circumstances and issues that remain obscure to historians. As bishop

of Lycopolis, Meletius appears to have taken advantage of Peter's absence from Alexandria during the Diocletianic persecution, seeking in 305 to gain control of the ecclesiastical power centered in Alexandria. After his censure the next year, Meletius ran afoul of civil authorities, and was sent to the mines in Palestine, enhancing his reputation with followers, who seem to have represented a more rigorist brand of Christianity. Meletius ordained bishops in Palestine and in Egypt (after his return) so that the Meletian church (with 28 bishops) was a group sufficiently problematic to church unity to be placed on the agenda at Nicaea in 325. For fuller treatment of the schism see H. I. Bell, *Jews and Christians in Egypt* (London, 1924) and E. R. Hardy, *Christian Egypt: Church and People* (New York, 1952), pp. 53ff. Not to be confused with this series of events is the Meletian schism that erupted in Antioch in 325, and drew its name from another Meletius, whose election to the episcopate there in 360 was a focus of dispute between parties in the later Arian controversy. See S. L. Greenslade, *Schism in the Early Church* (London, 1953), pp. 51–56, 227–228.

128. Antony's denunciation of Arian doctrine echoes other passages in Athanasius's polemical writings: the Son of God is not a creature, but always coexisted with the Father as the eternal Word and Wisdom from his essence. For parallel Athanasian descriptions of, and responses to, the ideas of Arius and his allies, see Athanasius *Or. c. Ar.* 1.9; *Ep.* 52; *Ep. Aeg.* 13.

129. 2 Cor. 6:14.

130. Rom. 1:25.

131. For an interpretation of the Arian scheme of salvation, and the importance of Christ's status as creature in it, see Gregg and Groh, *Early Arianism.*

132. The text suggests that Athanasius here gives a firsthand report of Antony's presence in Alexandria, a visit that is thought to have occurred in 337 or 338. The fact that only in this instance do we find a "we-passage" points to the possibility that Athanasius's contact with the monk was less frequent than the introduction of the *Life* might lead a reader to suppose; Athanasius would have made himself an eyewitness to the feats he describes, had he been able to do so credibly.

133. Origen's *Contra Celsum* 4.2.3 provides a glimpse of the enlightened pagan theologian's reservations about the idea of incarnation: Celsus asks why any such descent was necessary, since God could

teach or correct humans "by divine power without sending someone specially endowed for the purpose." The translation is by H. Chadwick, *Origen: Contra Celsum* (Cambridge, 1965) p. 186. Athanasius's more elaborate treatment of the issue is found in *De Incarnatione*, particularly in chaps. 11–16.

134. See Plotinus *En.* 5.1.3 and Philo *V. Mos.* 3.13. In these remarks unlettered Antony reveals his awareness of Neoplatonic thought, using terminology familiar from the writings of Plotinus. See A. H. Armstrong, "Plotinus," in *The Cambridge History of Later Greek and Early Medieval Philosophy* (Cambridge, 1967) pp. 195–268.

135. A fuller Athanasian treatment of pagan theology and piety is found in his treatise *Contra Gentes*, especially chaps. 9ff.

136. The Greek text in Migne does not inspire confidence. "Acclaimed" translates *euphēmoumena* (rather than *eusēmounema*). *Perikleiōmena* is understood here to derive from *kleiō* (= *kleō*), which connotes celebrity (see LSJ, kleiō [B], p. 957).

137. 1 Cor. 2:4.

138. Constantine was Caesar from 306–308, Augustus from 308–337; Constantius ruled as Caesar from 324–337, and as Augustus from 337–361; Constans was Caesar from 333–337, Augustus from 337–350. For a brief account of Constantine and his house, see A. H. M. Jones, *The Decline of the Ancient World* (London, 1966), chapters 4 and 5. For Constantine's role in ecclesiastical affairs, see the same author's *Constantine and the Conversion of Europe* (New York, 1962).

139. Cf. Heb. 1:2.

140. Dan. 4:16.

141. Serapion was the bishop of Thmuis in the Nile delta from about 340–360. For his importance in church affairs, see J. Quasten, *Patrology*, 3 (Antwerp, 1966), pp. 80–85.

142. Mt. 17:20.

143. Jn. 16:23–24.

144. Mt. 10:8.

145. See Mt. 7:2.

146. The story of Balacius is told differently in Athanasius's *Hist. Ar.* 14. There the letter is sent to Bishop Gregory and passed on to Balacius, who is bitten not by Nestorius's mount, but by his own. The mention of Gregory's episcopate (which ended with his death in 345) and of the prefecture of Nestorius (which began that year) places the

NOTES

"mishap" in that year. It remains puzzling why the two accounts differ in detail. Did Athanasius receive more information about the incident prior to writing the more extended version in the *Life of Antony?*

147. Christians as well as pagans practiced mummification and parlor display of the deceased, and this is what Antony repudiates prior to his death. See P. D. Scott-Moncrieff, *Paganism and Christianity in Egypt* (Cambridge, 1913), pp. 105 and 206.

148. Palladius gives the names of the men as Macarius and Amatus in the *Lausiac History*, ch. 21.

149. See Josh. 23:14.

150. Lk. 16:9.

ATHANASIUS'S *LETTER TO MARCELLINUS*

1. In speaking of Marcellinus's *askēsis*, here translated "discipline," Athanasius is probably referring not to "spiritual life" generally, but to monastic life in particular.

2. 2 Tim. 3:16.

3. The Triteuch (or "three volumes") consists of the books of Joshua, Judges, and Ruth.

4. Esdras = Ezra.

5. Ps. 113:1–2.

6. Ps. 104:26–31.

7. In the Septuagint, the superscription of Psalm 28 contains the words *exodiou skēnēs.*

8. Psalm 125 is one of those with the heading: *Odē tōn anabathmōn.*

9. Cf. Gen. 1:3ff.

10. Ps. 32:6.

11. Two aspects of Gnostic Christian belief are ruled out in this sentence: (1) docetic Christology, which envisioned the Savior in the guise of fleshly humanity while he remained supra-corporeal, and (2) the dissociation of Christ from the creation of the world, which in Gnostic circles was a work attributed to the Demuirge, a lesser being.

12. The usual reading of Psalm 86:5 in the Septuagint yields a different meaning: *A man shall say, Sion is my mother; and such a man was born in her; and the Highest himself has founded her.*

NOTES

13. Jn. 1:1, 2, 14.

14. Lk. 1:28.

15. Ps. 44:10.

16. Athanasius takes Isaiah's words not from the Septuagint, but from Mt. 8:17.

17. The Septuagint reads: *O Lord, you shall recompense them on my behalf.*

18. Hab. 3:1, which commences the poetry of the latter half of the book, reads: *Proseuchē Ambakoum tou prophetou meta ōdēs (a prayer of the prophet Ambacum, with a song).*

19. See 1 Cor. 12:4ff.

20. Is. 1:16 and Jer. 4:14.

21. See Dan. 12.

22. See Is. 36–37.

23. Ps. 36:8.

24. Ps. 33:14.

25. Athanasius suggests that hearing the Psalms produces a triple effect: One learns the history and prophecies available in other biblical books; beyond that, the Psalter cultivates the emotions, both by stirring and modulating them; hearing the Psalms consequently allows a conceptualization that is fuller than the initial understanding—a comprehension of the image produced by the phrases in a psalm that uniquely involves the hearer as the psalm's speaker and actor. This last aspect is elaborated in chapters 11 and 12 of the letter.

26. Reading *apechesthai* in place of the erroneous *upechesthai* in the Migne text.

27. Rom. 5:3, 5. The phrase *tē psychē* is an addition by Athanasius.

28. Cf. 1 Thess. 5:18.

29. Cf. 2 Tim. 3:12.

30. This passage in Athanasius's letter contains a number of difficulties and grammatical obscurities. The essential point, however, is clear: In comparison with other books in Scripture, certain of the Psalms possess an immediacy that enables the reader to appropriate their words as his or her own.

31. Athanasius's allusion is not altogether clear. See the similarly problematic phrase in Phil. 3:1, and also Rom. 12:11.

32. 3 Kings 17:1; 4 Kings 3:4 (EB: 1 and 2 Kings).

33. Ex. 33:13.

34. Ex. 32:32.

NOTES

35. For the phrase *elegchomenos hypo tou suneidotos,* see Philo *De Jos.* 48; *Spec. Leg.* 3, 54.

36. Mt. 11:29.

37. 1 Cor. 11:1.

38. Athanasius's remarks stand within a long and embattled tradition of defense of the free moral activity of rational beings. Against philosophers' fatalist schemes that seemed to undermine the pursuit (and reward!) of virtue, Christian apologists stressed the importance of free choice (as in Justin, *Apol.* 43). It was in opposition to the supposed dogma of some Gnostic Christians that beings possessed predetermined "natures" that dictated the level of their spiritual capacity and of their behavior that Irenaeus (see, e.g., *Adv. Haer.* 1.1.11–12, 1.6.2–4), Origen (*De prin.* Preface [5], 1.5, 8; 2.8–11; 3.1), and others developed the insistent arguments concerning the moral autonomy of rational creatures. By the fourth century, the idea has come to be the theological, or anthropological, commonplace Athanasius here repeats. On the question of "natures" in Gnostic teaching, see F. Sagnard, *La Gnose valentinienne et le temoignage de Saint Irenee* (Paris, 1947), and the fine reappraisal of the issues involved in E. Pagels, *The Johannine Gospel in Gnostic Exegesis* (New York, 1973).

39. 1 Kings 23:13ff. (EB: 1 Sam. 23:13ff.).

40. 1 Kings 24:3.

41. Reading *chrēsimous* for *chrēsmous.* The term *stēlographia (memorial)* is in the superscription of Ps. 56.

42. *Adoleschia* has this sense in Ps. 54:2.

43. The early rising is noted in the psalm's opening line.

44. Ps. 63:7.

45. Athanasius, in *exp. Ps.* 113:7, signifies Christian churches by *ta aiōnia skēnōmata (eternal tabernacles).*

46. The heading specifies that Psalm 47 is *deutera sabbatou.*

47. Again, Athanasius paraphrases language found in the LXX heading of the psalm: *When the house was built after the captivity, a song of David.*

48. Phil. 3:14.

49. These psalms are headed by the *Allelouia.*

50. For the parts of the soul, see Plato *Rep.* 4:439ff., and T. M. Robinson, *Plato's Psychology* (Toronto, 1970). Also, Origen, *De Princ.* 3.4.1.

146

NOTES

51. Jn. 18:38.
52. Cf. 1 Cor. 2:16.
53. Jas. 5:13b.
54. Ps. 41:6, 11.
55. Ps. 72:2.
56. Ps. 117:6.
57. Ecclus. 15:9.
58. Cf. Rom. 8:13.
59. Heb. 11:33–36a.
60. Phil. 3:16.
61. See Deut. 31:19ff.
62. Deut. 17:18–19.
63. See Josh. 8:9ff.
64. 4 Kings 22:8ff. (EB: 2 Kings 22:8).
65. Josh. 3:2ff. and 1 Kings 2–4 (EB: 1 Sam. 2–4).
66. Acts 19:14–16.
67. Lk. 8:28 and Mt. 8:29.
68. Acts 16:18.
69. Lk. 10:17.
70. 4 Kings 3:15 (EB: 2 Kings 3:15).
71. Ps. 118:6.
72. Ps. 118:54.
73. Ps. 118:92.
74. 1 Tim. 4:15.

Index to Preface,
Introduction and Notes

nature of, 18–19, 133; and
prophecy, 23; and
salvation, xvi, xvii, xix,
xx, 12, 13, 24; and
Scripture, xviii; works of,
xv, 12, 133.
Christianity, and
asceticism, 6, 10, 132;
community of, 4, 7, 22;
and free choice, 146;
history of, 3, 4; ideal of,
6, 7; spirituality of, 6, 22.
Christology, of Arians, xvii,
12, 13, 136; and
Athanasius, xvii, xviii,
xx, 12, 13; docetic, 144.
Church, controversy, xi,
131, 142; and
monasticism, 15.
Clement, xi.
Climacus, John, xv.
Colossians, 2:15, 137.
Constans, 143.
Constantine, 143.
Constantius, 143.
Conversion, xv, xvi, xvii,
xix, 1, 15, 16.
1 Corinthians, 1:24, 138;
2:4, 143; 2:16, 147; 4:5,
141; 4:6, 138; 9:27, 135,
141; 11:1, 146; 12:4 ff.,
145; 12:7, 137; 15:10, 135;
15:31, 136; 15:42, 136.

2 Corinthians, 2:11, 137;
6:14, 142; 10–12, 138;
12:3, 141; 12:4, 141; 12:10,
135; 13:5, 141.
Cross, F. L., 131.

Danielou, J., 137.
Daniel, 4:16, 143; 12, 145.
David, 24.
Deification, xvi.
Demiurge, 144.
Demons, 4, 7, 8, 9, 11, 12,
132.
Deuteronomy, 17:18–19,
147; 31:19 ff., 147.
Devil, xv.
Diocletian, 142.
Discipline, xvii, 6–11, 12,
20, 22, 133, 144.
Doctrine, xiii, 11, 13, 18,
22.
Dodds, E. R., 137.
Donatists, 140.
Dörries, H., 132, 133.

Easter, date of, 19.
Ecclesiastes, 19; 4:8, 136;
6:2, 136.
Ecclesiasticus, 1:24, 137;
15:9, 147.
Elijah, 135.
Elisha, 135.
Ellershaw, H., 19.

of, 4; and Antony, 5, 8,
14, 15, 16, 17; and ascent,
xv; and asceticism, 6, 7,
8, 10; centers of, 141; and
discipline, 6, 7, 144; and
isolation, 6, 8, 9, 15, 131,
138–139; revivals of, 16;
saints of, xiv, xv, xvi;
spread of, 16.
Montfaucon, Bernard De,
19.

Neoplatonism, 143.
Nestorius, 143.
New Testament, xix, 20, 22,
26.
Nicaea, Council of, xi, xvii,
xix, xx, 11, 12, 13, 142.
Numbers, 24:5–6, 139.

Obedience, 6, 12.
Old Testament, xviii, xix,
4, 20, 26.
Origen, xi, xviii, 137, 142,
146.

Pachomius, 15.
Pagels, E., 146.
Palladius, 13, 14, 133, 138,
141, 144.
Pantaenus, xviii.
Paphnutius, 141.
Paul, 6.

Paul the Hermit, 13, 17.
Persecution, 139, 140, 141,
142.
Peter, Bishop of
Alexandria, 140, 142.
Philippians, 3:1, 145; 3:13,
136, 141; 3:14, 146; 3:16,
147.
Philo, 143, 146.
Philostratus, 5.
Pine-Coffin, R. S., 134.
Plato, 146.
Plotinus, 143.
Polycarp, xiv, 139.
Ponticianus, xv, 14, 15.
Porphyry, 5, 133.
Prayer, xvii, 2, 7, 8, 9, 11,
133.
Prophets, 24.
Proverbs, 3:23, 137; 15:13,
141; 24:15b, 140.
Psalms, effects of, 145;
interpretation of, xi, xiii,
xviii, 19, 21, 22, 23, 24;
and salvation, xix, xx;
uniqueness of, 23, 24; use
of, xiii, xviii, xix, 1, 2, 22,
23; 1:6, 138; 9:6, 138; 19:7,
138; 26:3, 136; 28, 144;
32:6, 144; 33:14, 145;
35:10, 22; 36:8, 145; 37:13,
138; 38:1–2, 137; 38:14,
137; 41:6, 11, 147; 44:10,

Index to Texts

157

Arsinoë, 43.
Artemus, 86.
Ascension, 105, 123.
Asceticism, 64; and
Antony, 29, 32, 36, 37, 38,
42, 66, 94; and demons,
54, 57; and devil, 50; life
of, 29, 36, 37, 42, 45; need
for, 47; and sin, 73.
Assyrians, 53.
Athanasius, 97.

Balacius, 93–94.
Body, enslaving of, 73;
mortification of, 36;
pleasures of, 36, 65, 72;
and soul, 65.
Busirus, 74.

Carmel, Mount, 109.
Chaireu, 93.
Cham, 102.
Christ, and Arians, 82, 83,
97; calling on, 66, 89, 92;
coming of, 62, 85, 104,
123; cross of, 84–89; and
demons, 70, 88, 99; and
devil, 34, 61, 62; devotion
to, 54, 99; faith in, 44, 66,
84, 87, 88, 89, 92, 96, 99;
is God, 86, 88, 99, 104;
grace of, 50; incarnation
of, 85, 104, 105, 122; love

of, 38, 42, 61; name of,
61, 78, 83, 88, 92; piety
toward, 33; servants of,
70, 99; teaching of, 88, 92;
trust in, 87, 97; workings
of, 89; worship of, 90.
Christians, 30; and Arians,
82, 93; and demons, 47,
48, 49, 53, 62, 63; faith of,
99; and persecution, 66,
93; testing of, 48.
Chronicles, 102.
Church, excellence of, 120;
and knowledge of God,
119; persecution of, 65;
rule of, 81; and wrath,
91.
Commandments, 57, 72, 99,
102, 107, 108, 110, 128.
Compassion, 117.
Confessors, 66.
Conscience, 111; purity of,
60, 80.
Consolation, 118, 119.
Constans Augustus, 89.
Constantine Augustus, 89.
Constantius Augustus, 89.
Conversion, 87.
Courage, 58, 59, 63, 85, 119.
Cross, and Greeks, 84–89;
of Lord, 57; power of, 89;
and Psalms, 105, 123;
sign of, 41, 57, 70, 88.

Faith, act of, 87; of
    Antony, 34, 81; in Christ,
    44, 66, 84, 87, 88, 89, 92,
    96; contests of, 66;
    effective, 87; encouraging
    of, 43; in God, 87, 122;
    keeping of, 57, 128; in
    Lord, 39, 48, 72, 74, 96,
    109, 121; men of, 74, 128;
    of monks, 71; and
    orthodoxy, 81; and
    persecution, 91; and
    Scripture, 112; spreading
    of, 87.
Fasting, 33, 34, 48, 51, 54,
    61, 66.
Father, judgment of, 106;
    kingdom of, 65;
    petitioning of, 92; power
    of, 58; and Savior, 123;
    and Son, 82, 104; and
    soul, 85; and Word, 82,
    103, 104.
Fronto, 74.

Gabriel, 58, 59, 104.
Gaul, 99.
Genesis, 102.
Gentiles, 106, 110, 123.
Giezi, 57.
Glory, 44; of God, 102, 103,
    120, 122; of Lord, 61, 78,
    99, 103.
God, calling to, 116, 119,

120, 127; and creation, 47;
    and demons, 51; design
    of, 31; desire for, 117;
    devotion to, 39, 79; fear
    of, 54, 92; foreknowledge
    of, 55, 57; grace of, 34;
    and healing, 73, 129;
    honor of, 52, 103; house
    of, 120; image of, 54;
    inspiration of, 42;
    kindness of, 118, 122;
    knowledge of, 87, 88, 119;
    love for, 59, 124; love of,
    33, 42, 93, 98, 117; man
    of, 83, 98, 99; pleasing of,
    57, 125, 127; power of, 58,
    87; praise of, 83, 117, 118,
    119, 120, 121, 123, 125;
    providence of, 37, 115,
    121; servant of, 93, 120;
    sons of, 103; thanks to,
    73, 78, 108, 109, 111, 119,
    121; trust in, 54, 127; will
    of, 37, 73, 124; works of,
    45; worship of, 59, 86, 87,
    106, 120; wrath of, 119.
Gospels, 31, 45, 54, 58, 121.
Greeks, 46, 112, 119; and
    Antony, 83–89; and
    demons, 59, 99; oracles
    of, 56.

Habakkuk, 106.
Heart, and demons, 48; and

fear, 38; purity of, 37; rejoicing of, 81; turned to God, 46; watchfulness of, 47.

Heaven, citizens of, 43; desire for, 65; hope for, 31, 44; journey to, 47; kingdom of, 44, 46, 99, 115; names written in, 60; third, 79.

Hephaestus, 86.

Hera, 86.

Heresy, 82, 97, 117, 119.

Holy Spirit, 35; gifts of, 48; grace of, 107; as guide, 129; and Scripture, 105, 106, 107, 111, 127; and soul, 124, 125, 126.

Hope, against enemies, 120; in God, 108, 111, 115, 117, 120; for heaven, 31, 44; in Lord, 37, 63, 118, 125; in soul, 63.

Isaac, 110.

Isaiah, 105, 106, 107.

Isis, 86.

Israel, 64, 110, 122, 128; exodus of, 102; God of, 46; journeying of, 107; tribes of, 103.

Jacob, 30, 64, 81, 102.

Jerusalem, 103, 107.

Jews, 105, 114, 121, 123, 124, 129.

Job, 49, 53–54, 63.

John the Baptist, 46, 59.

Joshua, 46, 103, 128.

Josiah, 128.

Judas, 45, 63, 123.

Judea, 102.

Judges, 103.

Judgment, 34, 57, 92; coming, 90; Day of, 46; of Father, 106; of God, 75, 106, 116; of Lord, 121, 123; and Scripture, 128.

Kingdom, of Father, 65; of God, 46, 104; of heaven, 44, 46, 99, 115.

Kings, 102.

Kronos, 86.

Laban, 81.

Laodicea, 77.

Law, 35, 89, 96, 115, 124, 128, 129.

Life, amendment of, 99; of asceticism, 29, 36, 37, 42, 45; conduct of, 47, 49, 52, 57, 60, 109, 129; of discipline, 41, 43, 76, 77; eternal, 43, 44; just-, 54; knowledge of, 37; present, 43, 44, 45, 65; of

161

162

30, 113, 116; 31, 113, 114, 117; 32, 113, 117; 33, 113, 117; 34, 113, 116; 35, 113; 36, 113, 117; 37, 113, 114; 38, 114, 117; 39, 114, 117; 40, 113, 114, 117; 41, 114, 117; 42, 113, 116; 43, 113, 118; 44, 104, 113, 123; 45, 113, 118; 46, 105, 106, 113, 123; 47, 114, 120; 48, 113; 49, 103, 106, 113, 123; 50, 111, 118; 51, 113, 118; 52, 113, 115; 53, 111, 113, 118; 54, 113, 118; 55, 111, 113, 118; 56, 111, 113, 118; 57, 114, 118; 58, 113, 118; 59, 113; 60, 113; 61, 114, 119; 62, 113, 119; 63, 113, 114, 119; 64, 114, 119; 65, 114, 119; 66, 119; 67, 113; 68, 105, 113, 123; 69, 113, 119; 70, 113, 119; 71, 105, 106, 123; 72, 113, 119; 73, 113, 119; 74, 113, 114, 119; 75, 113, 114, 119; 76, 113, 119; 77, 102, 118; 78, 113, 120; 79, 113; 80, 113, 120; 81, 106, 114; 82, 113, 120; 83, 114, 115, 120; 84, 113, 120; 85, 113, 115; 86, 104, 120; 87, 105, 115; 88, 113, 118; 89, 113, 115; 90, 120; 91, 113, 119, 120; 92, 120, 121, 122, 123; 93, 121; 94, 113, 120; 95, 113, 121, 122; 96, 113, 114, 121; 97, 113, 122, 123; 98, 114, 123; 99, 114, 121; 100, 121; 101, 113, 121; 102, 113, 121; 103, 113, 121; 104, 102, 113, 118, 119, 121, 122; 105, 102, 113, 118, 119, 122; 106, 103, 113, 118, 119, 121, 122; 107, 113, 119; 108, 113, 123; 109, 104, 106, 113, 123; 110, 113, 119; 111, 114, 122; 112, 122; 113, 102, 113, 118, 122; 114, 113, 114, 118, 122; 115, 113, 122; 117, 103, 113, 119, 122; 118, 113, 114, 122, 129; 120, 113; 121, 103, 113; 122, 113; 123, 113; 125, 103, 113, 120; 126, 113, 116; 127, 113, 114; 128, 113; 129, 113; 130, 113; 131, 131; 134, 121, 122; 135, 113, 119, 122; 136, 113, 122; 137, 105, 113, 119; 138, 113, 122; 139, 113, 122; 140, 115; 141, 111, 113; 142, 113, 122; 143, 113, 122; 144, 113, 122; 145, 113, 121, 122; 146, 113, 121, 122; 147, 121,

51, 82, 88, 89, 99, 104, 115; is Word, 104.

Soul, and confusion, 58, 63, 81; creation of, 85; delight of, 58, 59, 81; and faith, 49; and fear, 59, 63, 120; harmony of, 125, 126; and intellect, 34, 46, 65; light of, 58; and Lord, 47, 116; and mind of Christ, 124, 126; passage of, 80; purity of, 42, 57, 77, 81; state of, 42, 46, 57, 87, 126; suffering of, 63, 117; and vice, 46; zeal of, 36.

Spain, 99.

Spirits, discernment of, 48, 58, 59, 60, 64, 94.

Suffering, bearing of, 108, 115, 119, 126, 129; deliverance from, 103; from demons, 88; of Lord, 105, 123; patience in, 73.

Susanna, 107, 124.

Tabernacle, 102–120.
Tharsis, 106.
Thebaid, 55, 67.
Thebans, 40.
Theodore, 76.

Tripoli, 74.
Triteuch, 102.
Typhon, 86.

Virginity, 72, 88, 93, 95.
Virtue, of Antony, 98; boasting of, 60; discipline of, 29; love for, 52, 64, 99; of Savior, 112; and Scripture, 128; way of, 32, 36, 44, 46, 51, 99, 113; and will, 46.

Visions, of Antony, 39, 41, 75, 78–79, 90, 91; and fear, 58, 64; of good, 39; of holy ones, 58, 59, 64.

Wisdom, of Antony, 83, 89; of Greeks, 87; heavenly, 47; Son is, 82, 104.

World, beginning of, 101; separation from, 36, 94; worth of, 44.

Word, 82, 85, 103, 104.

Zacharias, 58, 59.
Zeal, and Antony, 32, 36, 40, 41, 68, 95; for evil, 117; men of, 32, 36, 71; for virtue, 99.
Ziphites, 118.